TRANSCENDENCE

TRANSCENDENCE

Edited by
HERBERT W. RICHARDSON
and
DONALD R. CUTLER

Beacon Press   Boston

TABLE OF CONTENTS

v

FOREWORD

This volume had its genesis in one of a series of symposia that the Church Society for College Work of Cambridge, Massachusetts, has been administering for the purpose of exploring themes of great intellectual and cultural import for our time. Certain of the symposia have yielded occasional pamphlets; in other cases the character of the theme and the nature of the writings evoked by the symposia have commanded the attention of publishing houses.

Late in 1967, and somewhat nervously, Myron D. Bloy, Jr., the executive director of the Church Society, sent out invitations to a symposium on "Transcendence in Contemporary Culture" on the grounds that ". . . we have chosen this theme because we assumed that one of the gross characteristics of the emergent technological culture is the mutation, if not the dissolution, of a viable sense of transcendence." Undismayed by the cautious tone of the invitation, a number of persons gathered at the Episcopal Theological School in Cambridge in December to plan an exploration of contemporary ideas about transcendence; among them were Robert Bellah, Harvey Cox, Dorothy Day, Emil Fackenheim, Abraham Maslow, Michael Murphy, Huston Smith, Myron Bloy, and I.

Several essays were commissioned and the group met again for a weekend in May of 1968 at Endicott House in Dedham, Massachusetts. Donald Schon, Daniel Callahan, William Coolidge, Hubert Dreyfus, Roger Johnson, and Ruel Tyson joined the original group either to present papers or to engage in the discussions.

The tone of this volume is dependent to a considerable extent upon the character of the symposium itself. The sessions were unusually candid, democratic, and humane. The quest for transcendence itself touched the quality of the discourse.

When the papers prepared for the symposium had been acquired for publication, we decided to augment them by adding a few other essays to establish more clearly the very extensive and promising boundaries of the discussion of transcendence today. One senses in the volume as published, then, that the cautionary note of the original invitation to the symposium was not borne out by subsequent work, and that contemporary quests for transcendence are legion, manifold, and compelling.

D. R. C.

INTRODUCTION
HERBERT W. RICHARDSON

THE STUDY OF TRANSCENDENCE is provoked by the quest for transcendence. At the Endicott House conference at which several essays in this volume were presented for criticism, the members watched a film Huston Smith had made of the ecstatic experience of Tibetan monks in northern India. Sitting at ritual meditation, the monks were able to utter unearthly music consisting of chords that each monk could himself sound. It was not music in parts; it was a choir each member of which was sounding the whole chord. When the film had ended and the music ceased to pervade the room, we sat for a time in the dark room in profound silence. Then quietly we made our way back to the seminar room, appropriately motivated to talk *about* transcendence for having experienced an episode in the quest for Transcendence.

The quest, of course, need not be that alien to everyday life in Western societies. Harvey Cox, one of the contributors to this volume, has noted in another context that there exists a kind of underground of books and readership in American universities. At any given time, a half-dozen or more titles will be popular among students as a relief from the regular curriculum. The specific preoccupations of the titles vary widely from the modes of pop art, on the one hand, and scientific investigations of communication between dolphins and human beings, on the other. To get on the underground list, however, a book has to be related to the urge to move from ordinary dimensions of action and consciousness to extraordinary dimensions of life. The flatness of much of the curriculum is supplemented by deliberate excursions to deeper or higher, depending on your own preference for metaphors, dimensions.

If there is a knack to pursuing transcendent experience, it may be a knack we habitually suppress. I remember well a moment several springs ago when my wife and I were snapping together the tops and bottoms of our two-year-old son's pajamas. The quietness at his crib was broken by the sound of an airplane flying toward, then over, and finally away from our house. My son listened intently to the sound. When the engine's noise had faded entirely westward, a look of amazement and wonderment appeared. "All gone!" he said.

Only the little children among us are still filled with wonder at the mere fact of being and not-being, still filled with awe when something appears suddenly out of the infinite void that surrounds us. I was not surprised by the airplane. I knew there was an airport west of us and I was familiar with some of the flight patterns. Within a web of reasonings I had compassed the infinities of time and space so that very little appeared unanticipated or disappeared unexpectedly. In those days I was a man of reason, Apollonian man, living without transcendence. Twenty-five years of reading, reciting, sitting in straight classroom rows, playing games according to the rules, and hearing "should" and "ought" and "responsible" had taught me how to construe the world rationally. Inwardly I was angry. I wanted to ask the single "Why?" and Apollonian man is never allowed to ask: "Why must I always ask 'why?' " To ask that question is to be a heretic. But something inside me kept pushing against the definition that bounded the infinity outside man by bounding the infinity inside him.

It occurred to me, however, that the experience that would evoke wonder in a grown, rational man might be an epiphany happening in us rather than an epiphany appearing before us. The More we seek, I believe, is a More we can beomce. We do not seek Transcendence in order to know it but in order to become it. Those who seek Transcendence to know, not to become, misuse reason. They construe arguments to imprison man within the limits of mortality; they marshal "ordinary language" in order to warn one against the impropriety of trying to speak of extraordinary experiences; they refer the idea of Transcendence to regrets about an intrinsic deficiency in man rather than to an intuition of man's essential wholeness.

Is the better way of tracking Transcendence to its lair through the shock of being or the shock of knowing? Is it something we are looking for, or a way of looking? This question is the theme of folk tales that preserve the unconscious wisdom of the human race. Recall, for example, the tale of the three wishes. You remember how it goes, that a person, unhappy in his condition, miraculously receives the gift of three wishes. After having twice chosen what he thought he had wanted, he uses the third wish with some relief to restore his life to its original, pre-wishes condition.

When I was young I dreamed how I could outwit the giver of the wishes. I planned when my turn came to request—with the first wish—an infinity of wishes. Thus insured against all future negative feedback, I would go on to establish a beatific kingdom. By the time the tale had been transmitted to me it taught the impossibility of the heart's ever reaching the object of its desire. The cynical wisdom of the third wish was to hold fast to the bird in hand. A useful teaching, I suppose, for those in authority as they try to dampen the enthusiasm of the utopians. But the secret of the tale shows through. Folk tales are a kind of Zen; they are koans that yield the wisdom of self-transformation. Even if I had had an infinity of wishes I would have wanted the classic third wish. Eventually I would have discovered that the More I wanted was not a something but another and different Me. The secret of the third wish is that a man returns to his original condition really wanting it. The goal of all his seeking is that he himself becomes the More.

Not all the contributors to this volume will agree with the position I have taken; the point of the undertaking is to delineate the basic insights and arguments about Transcendence that one finds in contemporary discussions. There are noteworthy elements of agreement, however, in most of the essays. The shared perspectives, some of them at least, may be stated as follows:

1. The writers presuppose the ultimacy or co-ultimacy of the historical-cosmic process, and assume that Transcendence is a reality intrinsically bound up with this process.

2. They assume the necessity of showing that the Transcendent, however conceived, must be *pragmatically* as well as (or instead of) *formally* true.

3. They evaluate Eastern religion and experience positively and draw upon these as a resource for clarifying their ideas. Taken

together, these assumptions represent a major reorientation in thought and deserve a volume of exposition.

To conceive of "Transcendence" in relation to "process" is to relate two notions that classical Western philosophy has regarded as contradictory *in principle*. The general assumption of these essays that the preclassical emphasis on the ultimacy of process must somehow be combined with the classical emphasis on the ultimacy of the transcendent (assumed to be immutable and nonprocessive) is another evidence that we live in an axial moment when man's questions as well as his answers are being reconstructed.

The several essayists agree that in some important sense the future of man is open and the outcome of life processes around us is contingent upon the action and/or spiritualization of man. This does not mean that, following the "theologians of hope," they conceive of Transcendence simply as "the future." It would be more accurate to say that they present Transcendence as that which makes a meaningful future conceivable. Transcendence is still defined in a somewhat Greek way as a realm or state differentiated from sheer becoming. Contra the Greeks, the essayists do not define Transcendence as antitemporal. It is assumed that Transcendence is a dimension of reality that makes possible a meaningful appropriation of time.

For Charles Hartshorne, Transcendence is not the future of process but the unitary structures of process. For Cox and Donald Schon, Transcendence means that man can create novelties and insert them in the flow of history. For Robert Bellah Transcendence is an order of symbolic unities necessary for the organization of societies within the temporal flow.

The second perspective common to these essays is thinking about Transcendence pragmatically. The meaning and truth of Transcendence are established partly by showing what the concept implies operationally and behaviorally. Very abstract concepts can pass this test. What a pragmatic orientation excludes, however, is ending the investigation with theory before the operational-behavioral implications have been thoroughly explored. The pragmatic orientation has made it possible for the contributors to reconsider some traditional religious words. "Sin," "myth," "revelation," "spirit"—these words are not treated doctrinally. They are words for explaining human experience.

Thirdly, to dispel any notion that these "pragmatic" essays are parochial, one notes the high esteem the essayists express toward Eastern thought and mystical experience. Pragmatic America does have her own mystical tradition traceable from the Puritans through Emerson and the Transcendentalists to the many metaphysical religions of today. But that does not seem to account for our present interest in learning from the East. My own supposition is that this is one reflection of a major intellectual opening in America—an opening that may mean a more radical reorientation in outlook than the Enlightenment and the development of science, more radical because it is more discontinuous with our past intellectual and spiritual traditions.

Editorially, the essays in this volume are presented deliberately in pairs, and the reader may wish to read them two by two. The whole collection constitutes a broad variety of approaches to Transcendence, but each pair is matched to illumine two lines of thought which seem to clarify, correct, and complete each other as they lead the mind along two different lines toward the same object.

As a boon, a pinch of grace added to nature, the five sets of essays are preceded by a subtle analysis of conceptions of and ways toward the transcendent prepared by Huston Smith. This essay touches certain of the issues raised in this introduction and develops them in novel and persuasive ways. The novice should accept, as his first assignment, a careful study of this essay. It will, I believe, greatly enhance his intellectual perceptions and enable a more discriminating reading of those pieces that follow.

As a pair, the contributions of Michael Murphy and Sam Keen focus on the possibility of cognitive liberation, on the expansion of the self to new levels of experience, on the development of awareness to fourth, fifth, and sixth dimensions. Can man become psychologically and cognitively More than he has ordinarily been assumed to be? What are the inward possibilities?

The essays by Cox and Schon face outward toward the techno-historical process and the problem of control. Both writers see the increased velocities of history calling for a new definition of Transcendence and a new fantasy orientation that gives up entirely the Eden-dream of a Stable State.

The third pairing—the essays by Bellah and Richardson—tries to clarify the function of myths of transcendence as ordering structures in every society. Both essays explore the correspondence among theological, psychological, and sociological concepts.

In the fourth pairing one finds a more explicit interest in transcendence beliefs of traditional religions, Judaism in the case of Emil Fackenheim and Christianity in the case of Gordon Kaufman. Each seeks to clear the way for a positive revelation.

Because the conviction of all these essays is that ultimate reality is a process in some respect, we have added a final metaphysical discussion to the volume. Two eminent American philosophers, Henry Nelson Wieman and Hartshorne, discuss the implications for a concept of transcendence that follows from affirming the creative freedom of man. In these essays one sees the degree to which American thought has shifted away from the concept of immutability as a value.

When the world and reason were thought to be static and syllogistic, men sought to demonstrate the reality of the Transcendent by employing a single rational argument or by isolating an irreducible religious experience. The usefulness of such proofs has become dubious. The meaning of this state of affairs is a matter of philosophic dispute. But I suggest that it is more sensible to conclude not that proofs for the existence of the transcendent are impossible but that the nature of a decisive proof has changed.

Charles Sanders Peirce once pointed out that in a universe composed of multiple processes the most trustworthy affirmations grow out of an accumulation of slight arguments and evidences which tend to corroborate one another and point in the same direction. Demonstrations of proofs of this sort would be like great cables woven from many small wires, and different from strong chains constructed through the connections of single links. A cable's strength does not depend absolutely upon the strength of any one of its wires, but upon the synergistic multiplication of the strength and tendency of many strands. The chain snaps with a single major flaw.

The astute reader will find more than a single flaw in these essays.

That is granted—even encouraged. But that such discoveries will mean as much in our world as they meant for the mediaeval mind is denied. The tendency of these essays, considered altogether, is persuasive. In a peculiarly modern way, therefore, this collection might be regarded as a new form of what an earlier age sought to provide more simply: a demonstration of, and an incentive toward, God.

THE REACH AND THE GRASP: TRANSCENDENCE TODAY

HUSTON SMITH

MAN LIVES FOREVER ON THE VERGE, on the threshold of "something more" than he can currently apprehend.

This "more" presents itself most conspicuously in space. The center of the universe is where I happen to stand at any moment. From this center space spreads. I can move into it in any direction I please: forward or backward, right or left, even, with more difficulty, up or down. I lift my eyes and space stretches toward a horizon. If I try to approach this horizon, it recedes indefinitely, backstopped by light years.

In time, too, I sense myself enveloped by more than is evident. Moment by moment I slide from a past that is vanishing into a future that has yet to appear. Most of yesterday is gone already; tomorrow has not yet arrived. And beyond these proximate "befores" and "afters" stretch pasts and futures that may be infinite.

If we were content with the obvious we might stop here and regard man as a boundary creature only in these physical respects. Actually, however, our existence is endlessly liminal and adumbrative. Philip Wheelwright suggests that an entire "metaphysics of the threshold" might be needed to do justice to the ineluctable fact that as human beings "we are never quite *there*, we are always and deviously on the verge of being there."[1] The Marxist philosopher Ernst Bloch proposes a comparable "ontology of the not-yet-being" built on categories of possibility, the new, and futurity.[2] Though Asia is generally considered to be oriented to the past or present, she too looks toward More: "To feel . . . that all is at peace, to set ourselves down in a state of so-called satori, means there is as yet no real understanding of Buddhism. If we are really receptive to Buddhism

1

there is always the feeling of not enough, not enough; limitless endeavour and striving continued age after age, that must be the spirit of Mahayana."[3] Nietzsche's Zarathustra was right; "man is a bridge and not an end."

I propose to use "Transcendence" to name the *there* with respect to value which we sense as encircling our present existence; the Value More that exceeds our current possession; the presentiment that salvation, while not identical with our present stance, is nevertheless at hand.

Whether this Value More exists independent of and prior to our awareness of it, like space, or *per contra* is, prior to detection, only a possibility, like things that can but need not emerge in time—this question I shall finesse. Ontological realists, like Plato, espouse the former option; emergent evolutionists, like Bergson, the latter. The dispute isn't pointless, for if something already exists the prospect of laying hold of it seems greater than if we must take our chances on its coming into being in the first place. But if we read "possibility" here as "real possibility," equal in probability to the probability of our connecting with values that in some way do already exist, we can bypass the ontological dispute in favor of issues concerning Transcendence that are more metaphysically neutral.

Though the ontological status of the Value More can be left undetermined, other aspects of the category need to be pinned down. Each new moment adds *something* to our value store. If Transcendence designated only such an incremental "more" everyone would acknowledge its claims and the concept would cease to be interesting. Transcendence is not "more of the same." We do not encounter it in the form of another good dinner added to the list of all the dinners we have previously enjoyed. Even if the dinner is the best ever—or the experience, whatever its character, better than any to have previously come our way—Transcendence has not appeared. Experiences of Transcendence are probably of a very high order—"peak experiences" in Maslow's designation—but to *define* them by their position in a hierarchy of values lays one open to all the unresolvable difficulties of "hedonic calculus."

Transcendence should be defined neither quantitatively as "more of the same" nor qualitatively as "better than anything previously experienced" but in terms of the *kind* of value it designates. The effect of its appearance is to counter predicaments that are ingrained in the human situation; predicaments which, being not fully remediable, are constitutional.

What are these predicaments? Existentialists have described them adequately but have produced no résumé as compact as Gautama's "Three Signs of Being." As I wish to explore the transcendence of life's predicaments, not their description, I shall work with the Buddhist formulation. The predicaments which man must come to terms with in one way or another are:

a. *Dukkha*, suffering.
b. *Anicca*, transitoriness.
c. *Anatta*, no soul. Read "no personal significance." Individually we are nothing.

How does Transcendence counter these predicaments? To begin with, it counters them categorically rather than piecemeal. Dentistry remedies certain evils without affecting others. By contrast, transcendence, when it touches *dis*value, alters the entire field. It is a gestalt phenomenon, changing nothing within the field unless in some way it changes the field as a whole. Secondly, it counters *dis*-values paradoxically. Instead of eliminating them, it transmutes them. If a man hits his thumb with a hammer, the fact that he lives *sub species transcendentia* doesn't keep his thumb from hurting. Transcendence doesn't work on suffering like anaesthesia does, by simply blotting it out. The pain remains; it is the quality (significance, import) of pain that has been affected. Thirdly, transcendence effects its results noetically, through insight. Noetically here differs from emotively, through emotion. Emotion is involved, but it is consequent upon insight, like the joy brought on by the discovery that "she loves me." Thus, transcendence is a state of actual or potential being, the discernment of which counters categorically, paradoxically, and noetically the *dis*values of suffering, transience, and insignificance or futility (as implied by Ecclesiastes' "Vanity of vanities! All is vanity").

IMMANENCE

Before proceeding with Transcendence it is worth noting that there is one condition in which all talk of Transcendence is superfluous. This condition is Immanence, capitalized to indicate that it embodies all the values of Transcendence minus the sense that those values await realization. Elsewhere in this volume (p. 89) Robert Bellah quotes Wallace Stevens'

> . . . times of inherent excellence,

> As when the cock crows on the left and all
> Is well, incalculable balances,
> At which a kind of Swiss perfection comes. . . .[4]

Such moments of inherent excellence transcend the need for transcendence itself, for when one is totally fulfilled one asks for nothing more, neither that one live forever, nor that the past be eternally preserved, nor that one's life count; all such concerns, being extrinsic, disappear. Meister Eckhart wrote that while he was in the source of the Godhead no one asked him where he was going or what he was doing. "There was no one there to ask me." It was only after he emerged that "the world of creatures began to shout: 'God.'" That is the point. Only when Immanence dissolves does the world begin to shout "God" and the issue of Transcendence descends upon us.

Let us consider what Immanence does to transitoriness, leaving its parallel operations on vanity and suffering to be dubbed in by the reader. Immanence transfigures time into eternity. Peter Munz argues that all religion is essentially such "a search for the *salus* that consists in knowing how transience can be transcended."[5] "Man's greatest disease is the consciousness of transience. Nothing is so likely to produce despair as the awareness of the contingency and vanity of life. A powerful cure . . . is . . . a perception of eternity. . . . The theologian who helps us to this perception is the great physician."[6]

"Eternity" here doesn't denote everlastingness—continuance in time forever—but rather total presence in the present: Eckhart's "Now moment," Buddha's "single instant awakening," Wittgenstein's "He lives eternally, who lives in the present." It names those moments in time in which the present emerges as a single point in the stream that flows from the past into the future. Eternity is an instant in which past and future disappear.

Since our empirical ego is the sum total of the desires, urges, and plans that we pursue and satisfy in time, the transfiguration of time into eternity—the moment in which time gives way to the present—is concomitant with the transcendence of the empirical ego. Or perhaps it is better to put it the other way around; transcendence of the empirical ego transfigures time. Remorse drags us back into the past; worry projects us into the future. To be released from both is to be free to live in the present, like lilies of the field, taking no thought of the morrow. To live in eternity is to live from moment to moment; to live not in the realm of means but in the realm of ends in which every act is an end in itself and has no purpose beyond itself.

If eternity requires transcending the empirical ego, it also requires release from the idea of physical time which stands as a screen between ourselves and the present, blocking communion and forcing us to care and plan for a future in which we nevertheless know all our achievements will be transient. Only when physical time dissolves in the emptiness of *sunyata*—the void as the Buddhists would say—can we "find that sublime flavour, that direct experience, at each step in our path . . . step after step." [7]

When Buddhists speak of throwing away their rafts after their rivers have been crossed and the *Lankavatara Sutra* tells us that there is really nothing to be acquired, nothing to be delivered from; no Way, no Goal, no Round, no Nirvana, nothing at all needing to be done or undone; it is from this state of Immanence, realized or envisioned, that they speak. It is, as we have said, from *outside* this condition that Transcendence appears, in something like the way that oxygen jumps to notice when we lack it. It may be that the further a life or culture stands from intrinsic fulfillment, defined as desiring nothing to be different from the way it is,[8] the more prominently Transcendence will figure in its outlook, provided vitality doesn't decline. A related point would be: the further the remove from Immanence, the more dramatic the experience of Immanence if achieved. "The deeper the clinging to life, the more clearly is release known. The stronger the passions show themselves to be, the deeper the experience of the Buddha salvation."[9] If so, this would explain, for example, why apocalypticism appeared and reappeared in Judaism's most difficult periods. What we can say more confidently is that the *guise* in which Transcendence appears varies with the mode of life's deficiency. Those who suffer from bondage and confinement see it as promising liberation and expansion. Those who suffer from darkness look to it for light. To those who groan under the weight of death and transitoriness it intimates eternity. To those who are restless it betokens peace.

THIS-WORLDLY TRANSCENDENCE

The fact of Immanence proves that men do not always seek Transcendence. When they do they can either seek it within the world's confines—meaning the confines of reality as usually envisioned—or test to see if these confines are final. Transcendence within our normal worldview I shall call this-worldly Transcendence; outside it, ontological Transcendence.

1. *Love.* The clearest instance of this-worldly Transcendence is occasioned by love. Kierkegaard better than anyone else has explained the dynamics of this solution to the human problem. The self, being dichotomous (composed of two halves, finite and infinite, temporal and eternal) is incapable of uniting itself by itself. Only when something outside the self takes possession of it, causing it to become fully absorbed with this outside something, can the self's two parts be aligned. In living with the princess day by day, the swain fulfills the temporal half of his being; at the same time, she fulfills his need for eternity, for something that doesn't change and isn't in flux, by "gestalting" all the time in his life. This gestalt is experienced as constant and is in this sense eternal: the time before he encountered the princess was prelude, her entry into his life was decisive climax and everything subsequent has been consummation.

The dynamics are similar with respect to finitude and infinity. The princess fulfills the swain's finite yearning; he can touch her and delight in her beauty which is concrete and particular. But she fills equally his infinite need. She provides him with something (herself) to which he can give himself infinitely (totally, completely).

There is no questioning the effectiveness of this solution to man's dilemma. The problem is to keep it working, that is, to keep the swain's passion for the princess infinite. Berdyaev thinks most marriages are unhappy. One need not go with him that far to concede that few experience the clear-cut before-and-after effect respecting fulfillment that Kierkegaard wants. Romantic love can effect Transcendence, but once love settles into fondness and companionship it does no disrespect to what these add to human happiness to admit that at the level at which they usually function, they fail to keep people from wanting additional solutions to the human situation.

2. *Hope* can be one of the supplementing solutions. Hope redeems the present and makes it significant and enduring by tying it to a meaningful future. As with love, no one doubts that hope can counter *dis*values; one perceptive psychologist thinks that most human happiness actually derives from hopeful expectations concerning the future. St. Paul thought enough of hope's redeeming power to rank it with faith and love, and Georges Bernanos valued it enough in *Diary of a Country Priest* to consider sin against it the deadliest sin of all.

The question is not whether hope can redeem but whether it can be sustained. To youth, whose life consists more of promise than of actualization, hope exists naturally. Later, it is more difficult. Personal hope comes up against the question, with time running out and life possibilities narrowing in number, what reason is there to expect that the fulfillment (Transcendence) that hasn't reached me yet will come in the future? And collective hope that historical advances will improve the human condition across the board runs into the fact that each age seems to find itself with new problems as great as those recently solved.

These difficulties besetting hope in both its personal and collective expressions raise the question whether hope can in the long run be sustained within life seen through ordinary, mundane, objective eyes. This question is at the forefront of the current debate by philosophers and theologians, Marxists and Christians, on hope and the future, Ernst Bloch (*Das Prinzip Hoffnung*) representing one side and Jurgen Moltmann (*Theology of Hope*) the other.

The answer is probably, "Some can, others cannot." For those who cannot, hope requires "another world" and faith in its existence. Indeed, the deeper one explores hope the more it begins to *resemble* faith in some form. St. Paul lists the two (and love) separately, but this may be a theological variant of outmoded "faculty psychology." Psychologists used to treat mind, will, and emotion as distinct human faculties; today they are impressed by the overlap. It may be that the separation of faith, hope, and love is provisional only, and that to sustain the division is to produce "faculty theology." The closer one approaches life's vital center, the more human faculties converge.

3. *Commitment to a cause* represents a third avenue to this-worldly Transcendence. "Ah, if only one could die suddenly as he is serving a Purpose," Kazantzakis cries. In *The Devil and Daniel Webster,* Stephen Vincent Benét makes the same point less directly. Having been cheated out of Jabez Stone's soul by Webster's oratory and legal agility, the Devil offers to tell Webster's fortune, taking this opportunity to bury Webster's hopes.

The forecast is that Webster has a great ambition to be President but he will not succeed; lesser men will be chosen and he passed over. He wants to establish a dynasty, but both his sons will die in war. He is proud of his oratory, but his last great speech will turn many of his fellows against him; they will say he has turned his coat and sold his country, and their voices will be loud against him until he dies. Webster hears the Devil out and then puts one question to him: The Union, will it endure? When the Devil has to concede that it will, Webster retorts,

> Why, then, you long-barreled, slab-sided, lantern-jawed, fortune-telling note shaver . . . be off with you to your own place before I put my mark on you! For, by the thirteen original colonies, I'd go to the Pit itself to save the Union!

ONTOLOGICAL TRANSCENDENCE

Immanence, being self-contained, is the best mode of life, but it is difficult to sustain. This-worldly transcendence is occasioned by something within the ordinary world: a loved one, a specific hope, or a cause that commends itself as deserving. Such Transcendence works for everyone at times, and perhaps enough, for some to preclude their asking for any other mode. But there are others who do not find in Immanence or this-worldly Transcendence the fulfillment they seek.

Such persons exist and I think it as probable that their "this-worldly" discontent is divine (engendered by exceptional sensitivity) as that it is neurotic (the result of failure of nerve or warped childhoods). I extend my typology, therefore, to include ontological Transcendence, defined as Transcendence deriving from the possibility that reality houses reservoirs of value qualitatively different from what we normally perceive or assume. To pursue the possibility of Ontological Transcendence is, of course, to fly in the face of recent "secular theology," but this pursuit requires no apology. The secular theologians' request that we stop speaking of God as "out there" may be useful, for geography never applies literally to spiritual affairs. But their proposal that we drop all talk of a "behind the scenes" reality seems curious. Secular theologians tend to be science enthusiasts, yet "behind the scenes" sounds like precisely what the scientists have been uncovering as they penetrate deeper and deeper into nature's undersurface. In human experience, probability waves and antimatter aren't exactly at stage center.

Anthropologists generally agree that in situations of life crisis and emotional stress primitive man experienced rescue through myths that showed him a way of escape where empirically none had existed.[10] The need for such transempirical ways has not disappeared. Mankind continues to be cramped enough by the limits of worldly existence to warrant asking if there is conceivably a more commodious existence. We need not approach the question apologetically as if ontological Transcendence were a crutch for the maimed. Physicians are becoming interested in the concept of positive health, a state of well-being as much above what we consider normal health as disease falls below it. Transcendence has comparable creative possibilities. The sustained secret excitement implicit in the speech of Socrates and his friends throughout the Platonic dialogues is one example of ontological Transcendence working, in that case taking the form of the Idea of the Good, to heighten the vitality of men who before they caught sight of it were, at the very least, perfectly normal.

Immortality is one possibility which, if actual, would instance ontological Transcendence. Another possibility is that reality is personal, that, in William James' formulation, we can "legitimately say *thou* to the universe." Classical theism affirms that we are loved by personal reality. A third possibility would occur in relation to an impersonal perfection, so self-contained that it doesn't know men as individuals and hence is not directly concerned with their well-being. The power of such an impersonal perfection—Nirguna Brahman, Sunyata, Plato's Idea of the Good, the Godhead—to effect transcendence has often been challenged, but without warrant. If such a perfection exists, it could afford a vision so stupendous that to glimpse it would be to find one's attention totally riveted, slicked to its object, with no remainder left for oneself and such residual questions as whether one is known or loved.

I have nothing against any of these possibilities. They have been explored thoroughly for centuries, however. It is perhaps more promising to ask if there are other reasonable ways reality's "more" might be envisioned. I wish, of course, that I could induce other modes of Transcendence to disclose themselves directly; since revelations can't be engineered I must fall back upon reason's service: to provide propaedeutics. Negatively, reason can remove obstacles to accepting ontological Transcendence; positively, it can fashion conceptual forms through which such Transcendence can be convincingly imagined.

Via Negativa. Dionysius the Areopagite, Avicenna, Maimonides, and the mystics in general represent an important theo-philosophical tradition which claimed that the difference in kind between finite and infinite precludes man from knowing anything about God's nature save what it is not. Current epistemology holds resources for a comparable *via negativa*, but with a different slant. Whereas the burden of traditional negative theology was that the Transcendent is, in its nature, unknown, the contemporary version must be that there is an unknown, aspects of which may be Transcendent. This neo-"negative theology" doesn't prove Transcendence; however, it does make room for it.

From the radiant energy of the total electromagnetic spectrum, human eyes register only a slender band. Similarly, we hear only a fraction of sound waves. Radio, X-, and gamma rays don't register with our senses at all; in this respect they are like magnetic fields. Given different sense receptors, we would perceive an unimaginably different world. From a wide range of possible directions, life, it appears, has traversed one among innumerable possibilities; it is the world we experience.

So much for our senses, their relativity, and the correspondingly relative world they offer for perception. But the world of our *conception*, which we can know even if we cannot directly perceive it, has turned out to be equally relative. The physical world, which prior to the rise of modern science seemed to be the only world, now turns out to be macro, or middle-sized. It is enveloped by the megaworld of astronomy and contains the microworld of quantum physics.

Each of these three physical worlds—the mega, the macro, and the micro, set one within another like Chinese boxes—has a distinct logical structure and mechanics in part independent of hierarchies above or below. The megaworld is expanding, its space is curved, and its geometry is non-Euclidian. In the microworld, matter is mostly empty and can be massless (the photon and neutrino). It can function somewhat like a particle, wave, or force (the latter instanced by mesons which act like glue to hold protons and neutrons together in nuclei). It can have life spans under a ten-billionth of a second or, where more stable, it can execute disappearing acts, appearing only at certain points as it moves along a line. It can be created (from energy) or destroyed (when, for example, positive and negative electrons collide and disappear in photons of light), and it has its mirror image in antimatter.

There is no reason to presume that these three "worlds" are exhaustive. Scientists are presently looking for new worlds beyond mega and micro: a transstellar, gallactic space whose distinctive mechanics may explain the quasars brightness 10,000 times that of a billion suns; and a subquantum level where we expect to find the quarks. There are difficulties, of course. The deeper we burrow into the interstices of matter the stronger we find the bonds that unite its elements; indeed, their strength increases exponentially rather than arithmetically, which has led Philip Morrison to calculate that to break matter apart at its quantum level would, by present methods, require an accelerator larger than the earth itself. Presumably new methods will be found, in which case we will be exposed to matter acting in five distinctive ways in each of five distinguishable dimensions.

David Bohm thinks the total number of dimensions is infinite.

Recognition that the way matter behaves on the human scale is only a special instance of nature's total repertory does bear some relation to negative theology's goal of ventilating our views of reality, but in the end neither this nor the preceding point about the partiality of sensory knowledge touches the *value* question. Not even J. B. S. Haldane's hunch that "the universe is not only queerer than we imagine; it is queerer than we *can* imagine" or James Coleman's verdict that relativity theory isn't difficult to understand, only difficult to believe,[11] implies that what strains imagination or belief pertains to value. Instead of tailing science to reach value we must backtrack and show that in the interest of control science ultimately turns its back on values and meanings in favor of what can be known objectively.[12] In the long run the most important task for neo-"negative theology" is to demonstrate in detail that: 1) epistemologies are hyphenated to the purposes for which they are designed; 2) contemporary epistemology is vectored by science whose primary purpose is to control nature; and 3) since this purpose is partial, epistemologies tailored to it are correlatively partial and incapable in principle of doing justice to reality's full (specifically value) dimensions.

The aim of neo-"negative theology" is not to prove Transcendence, but rather to make room for Transcendence if it shows a disposition to enter through extrarational channels. This may be the greatest service reason can render faith in our age, namely, to loosen the clods of prevailing modes of thought which welcome so little the seeds of faith. "Only that life is worth living," Nietzsche has Zarathustra say, "which develops the strength and the integrity to withstand the unavoidable sufferings and misfortunes of existence without flying into an imaginary world." Granted. What, however, is imaginary, and what real but elusive? "One world at a time," we hear, and fair enough, but not half a world. Reason operates in contemporary life under such heavy unconscious conditioning from science that it might be good for us if at certain times, for certain purposes, we had a Western equivalent of the Zen *koan* to decommission reason, to simply knock it out, allay it, so it wouldn't get in our way.

Conceptual forms. Though this negative service may be the greatest contribution reason can make to ontological Transcendence at this time, reason can also do something positive. It can formulate conceptions consonant with (though not implied by) the most sophisticated contemporary information, in which Transcendence can with dignity take lodging if Transcendence presents itself. I call these formulations "conceptual forms" and think of them as complementing the symbols Robert Bellah finds "unavoidable but provisional" in man's confrontation with reality: poetic symbols like those Bellah extracts from Wallace Stevens, religious symbols, including God, Lord, Nothingness, and Nirvana.

I shall try three formulations which involve, respectively, a spatial image, a temporal image, and an image from neurophysiology.

A spatial image. Are the three usual dimensions of space exhaustive? Edwin Abbott's *Flatland* raised this question intriguingly, and Karl Heim has built a full-scale theology on the premise that they are not. Mathematicians refer to abstract "configurational space" and "Hilbert space" (where "quarks" rotate in special unitary transformation in six dimensions); their work moves from three to four to "n" dimensions without hesitation. Physicists speak of electrons that disappear, then reappear elsewhere. Could this involve dropping out of our space and subsequent reentry? Hoyle's "continuous creation of matter-energy in space" has had to be greatly modified, but the conception must still be reckoned with; could matter-energy enter from another dimension?

What is the value-import of additional dimensions? If a dot extended through time produces a line, a line extended through time in a different dimension produces a plane, and a plane extended through time in still another dimension creates a solid, by extrapolation a solid extending through time in a fourth dimension would produce a four-dimensional body. As our sight is three-dimensional, we couldn't see such a four-dimensional body any more than two-dimensional sight could see an elongating block; to two-dimensional sight its advancing surface would appear as no more than a moving plane. *Mutatis mutandis:* if there *are* additional dimensions, our three-dimensional sight doesn't preclude us from having four-dimensional bodies created by the summation of all the past moments we have lived.

Conceptually, such a body might be described as the sum of all its intersections in three-dimensional space as it passes through time. We couldn't hope to visualize it, but William Witherspoon has suggested that imagining the dimension might be likened crudely to reconstruing a moving picture film of a bud opening into a full-blown flower. If we cut apart each frame of such a film, stacked the whole film together frame by frame, and then looked at the unfolding flower simultaneously through all the frames, that might be the most we could do to appease our yen for imagining the fourth dimension.

The concept of a four-dimensional figure would, of course, apply to a physical object, animate or inanimate. But if we have gone this far, there is no need to stop. Living things might differ from the nonliving by their involvement in a fifth dimension. Death, then, would be the cessation of movement in the fifth dimension while the corpse continued its movement in the fourth. Spirit, as distinct from life alone, could be the product of a sixth dimension. A four-dimensional body would expand to a fifth dimension by being alive and to a sixth if it were evolving spiritually. Ample dimensions remain, of course, for God.

It may be no accident that William Pollard, a theologian-physicist—as theologian, sensitive to value questions; as physicist, schooled in the extent to which reality differs from common sense—finds this spatial image meaningful. For the rest of us, time may lubricate our imaginings better than space.

A temporal image. Whatever one may think of the specifics of *The Phenomenon of Man*, the reception accorded that book indicates that Teilhard de Chardin tapped an immense potential in the contemporary mind for expanding its value perspective through the imagery of time.

Evolution was first a historical concept. It was applied next to biology and then to cosmology. We live not only in an expanding universe but in a universe that is evolving. This notion affects value most directly through the evolution of consciousness. At every stage evolution has brought to view a world which qualitatively as well as quantitatively would have been completely inconceivable from the vantage point of the preceding rung on the evolutionary ladder. What reason is there to suppose that we have reached the apex?

If the emergence of memory counters transience to some extent, might a further development not counter it more? If human consciousness enables us to step back from consciousness one step in *self*-consciousness, might not further developments enable us to step back a second step into ecological-consciousness and a third into cosmic-consciousness, thereby progressively countering insignificance? Perhaps we can no more imagine what such expanded states of consciousness would feel like than a dog can imagine what it would feel like to be self-conscious or to think abstractly. On the other hand, those moments when we sense within us "a self that touches all edges" (Wallace Stevens again) could be foretastes of a future which today man can sustain no longer than proto-amphibians could endure unhydrated oxygen.

A neurophysiological image. The human brain contains over 10 billion cells. Any single cell can be connected with up to 25,000 other cells. The possible paths through the cortical computer exceed the number of atoms in the universe. Something like a billion impulses flood up to it each second. A huge constriction process seems to work to reduce this prodigious information-processing device to manageable proportions. This is as it should be, for if we had to attend to a billion optional things, we might not attend sufficiently to the few things that require our attention if we are to survive: cars that bear down on us, pantries that need restocking, and the like.

If we had to nominate a group that faces in the rawest form life's three *dis*values as enumerated at the start of this essay, terminal cancer patients would be a logical choice. Their suffering tends to be acute and unrelieved. Their time is fast running out, and with it their personal significance. When their neural circuitry is rerouted by LSD, however, surprising things happen in about fifty per cent of the cases. The following descriptions are quoted from Sidney Cohen's "LSD and the Anguish of Dying":

> The pain is changed. I know that when I pressed here yesterday, I had an unendurable pain. I couldn't even stand the weight of a blanket. Now I press hard—it hurts, it hurts all right—but it doesn't register as terrifying.

> I could die now, quietly, uncomplaining—like those early Christians in the arena who must have watched the lions eating their entrails.

> I see that the hard deaths too, must be borne—like the difficult births, it is a part of you.

> When I die I won't be remembered long—there aren't many friends and hardly any relatives left. Nothing much accomplished—no children—nothing. But that's all right, too.[13]

Has the chemical recircuiting anaesthetized these patients or opened the doors of perception to enable them to see more of reality, or reality more objectively, than they and we normally do?

CONCLUSION

There seem to be two routes to human fulfillment, psychological and ontological. The former accepts more or less standard views of reality and seeks psychological resolution within those limits; when successful the result is either Immanence or this-worldly Transcendence, the difference being that in the latter fulfillment derives from something specifiable, a loved one, hope, a cause, or whatever. Ontological Transcendence, for its part, accepts the permanence of psychological tensions that cannot be resolved within reality as normally conceived, and so presses the possibility that reality includes surprising corridors of worth that elude ordinary eyes. Things are as they seem; things are not as they seem: that is the great divide.

This essay takes no position as to which side is right. The two types of fulfillment are equal both in worth and in difficulty. It is precisely as difficult to maintain genuine faith in ontological Transcendence as to achieve Immanence or this-worldly Transcendence. With respect to ontological Transcendence, my claim is not that it is superior or easier but that it *is* legitimate. There is no more reason to assume that reality conforms to the "man in the street's" suppositions of its worth than that it conforms to his notions of its physical complexity. A further claim is that the creation of conceptual forms through which man's imagination can grapple with ontological Transcendence is a useful enterprise. More important than the individual's right to believe, which concerned James, is his capacity to believe. Conceptual forms cannot deliver this capacity, but like background advertising, they can work the soil. The distinctions that have structured the paper—between Immanence and Transcendence, between this-worldly and ontological Transcendence, between psychological and ontological fulfillment—are probably themselves provisional. But this is not the last analysis; it is an analysis of where our thinking stands today.

REFERENCES

1. *The Burning Fountain* (Bloomington: Indiana University Press, 1968), p. 272.
2. See *Philosophische Grundfragen. Zur Ontologie des Noch-Nicht-Seins* (Frankfurt: Suhrkamp Verlag, 1961).
3. Trevor Leggett, ed., *The Tiger's Cave* (London: Rider and Co., 1964), p. 64.
4. Wallace Stevens, *Collected Poems* (New York: Alfred A. Knopf, 1955), p. 786.
5. *Problems of Religious Knowledge* (London: SCM Press, 1959), p. 22.
6. *Ibid.*, p. 129.
7. Leggett, *op. cit.*, p. 69.
8. Cf. Hakuin's Song of Zazen:
   At this moment what do you lack?
   As Nirvana presents itself before you,
   The place where you stand is the Land of Purity,
   And your person, the body of the Buddha.
9. Leggett, *op. cit.*, p. 90.
10. B. Malinowski, *Myth in Primitive Psychology* (London: Norton, 1926), pp. 23ff.
11. *Relativity for the Layman* (New York: William-Frederick, 1954), p. 48.
12. Cf. Munz, *Problems of Religious Knowledge, op. cit.*, pp. 128–129: "The scientist approaches the world with a well-defined aim. He wishes to understand the world so that he can manipulate it. This aim guides his investigations. He has framed the concept of truth in such a way that he can apply it to that kind of knowledge which enables him to manipulate events."
13. *Harper's Magazine*, September 1965.

EDUCATION FOR TRANSCENDENCE
MICHAEL MURPHY

IN AMERICA TODAY there is a widespread and growing interest in various psychophysical disciplines which evoke transcendent experience. Some of these disciplines, such as "transcendental meditation" or Zen training, are explicit about their transcendent aims. Others, such as techniques for increasing sensory and kinesthetic awareness or the various group encounter formats, describe their aims in terms of "personal growth," increased sensitivity, and awareness, or some other psychological or physical outcome. But these latter disciplines regularly evoke ego-surpassing, often ecstatic experience which is identical in crucial ways to the experience sought by the more explicitly contemplative methods.[1]

All of these disciplines—whether explicitly seeking Transcendence or not—share certain salient features. They all focus attention upon unfamiliar aspects or possibilities of one's world; they all attempt to break perceptual constancies; they all require surrender at crucial moments to alien and formerly resisted perceptions or feelings; and they all engender increased vitality and joy and a greater sense of meaning, freedom, and power when their practice is successful. Common to the practitioners of all of them is the sense that a fuller reality has made itself known, that something more has entered one's being, that a grace has been bestowed. In T-groups, sensory-awakening sessions, psychodramas and gestalt therapy, as well as in prayer or meditation, personal boundaries expand, often in ecstasy. This feeling of being entered by, or entering upon, something greater is at heart of the sense of Transcendence.

One reason for the silence regarding the transcendent aspect of this kind of contemporary experience is that the jargon of psychotherapists, group dynamics experts, and sensitivity trainers does not include categories to deal with it; modern psychology and sociology generally relegate Transcendence to an inferior order of reality. Another reason is that most contemplative traditions and the con-

18

temporary disciplines derived from them relegate many sensory and interpersonal illuminations to an inferior status, insisting that *satori*, or union with God, be achieved through a particular method and be expressed in a particular way. The cults that have' formed around such teachings are generally critical of any other path.[2] Narrowness on both sides keeps the picture incomplete.

But in spite of the inadequacies of modern psychological theory and traditional religious formulations, disciplines and centers are emerging all over the United States to stimulate and nurture self-transcending personal growth, and from them the beginnings of a contemporary education for Transcendence are coalescing. Severin Petersen, a research associate at the Esalen Institute, has catalogued over one hundred and fifty such disciplines, and in the past two years at least fourteen such centers have been organized. Theory to match this practice will emerge when Transcendence is assigned a fundamental reality and when it comes to be seen as multidimensional and inclusive of all man's parts rather than as the specialized, ascetic phenomenon it has generally been conceived to be by traditional religious thought. Beginnings have been made toward such relevant and inclusive formulations by Abraham Maslow and Dr. R. D. Laing, for example, by Aldous Huxley in his last essays and in the novel *Island* (in which he outlined an education for man, the "multiple amphibian"), and by Bishop John Robinson in *Exploration into God*.[3] Following Robert Bellah's suggestion, I think contemporary notions of Transcendence must be democratic rather than hierarchical and authoritarian. The Net of Jewels in Hindu mythology, in which every facet of existence mirrors every other facet, is a better symbol for the consciousness of our times than the image of a three-story psyche to be climbed with a narrow ladder of perfection.[4]

In spite of these new beginnings, however, the still-dominant intellectual attitude in the Western world does not esteem Transcendence as other cultures have. Instead, recent Western culture has prized science, social order, and control of the natural world. In America most persons would rather conquer the moon than explore the worlds of subjective experience and personal relationship.

Nowhere is this attitude more obvious than in our educational system. Upon entering school, our children must adapt to the various demands of classroom efficiency. They are taught to behave "normally," to think rationally and objectively, to relate verbally, and to control rather than cultivate their feelings. They may graduate as good citizens, well educated in the cognitive disciplines and well prepared to function as components in society, yet be strikingly unaware of themselves or others.

Such is the price, some say, of our progress. Others, however, are now declaring that the price may not be worth paying. On college campuses throughout America, students are demanding that they be taught not only to think, but also to feel. Many of them are insisting that a basic concern for ultimate values be added to their curricula and are turning meanwhile to psychedelic drugs. Eastern philosophy, and social action.

This new concern is paralleled by a growing interest in transcendental experience within the scientific community. In recent years, studies by Western psychologists have linked such experience with human growth and learning. Some educators and social scientists have begun to reevaluate Transcendence and to develop techniques which evoke and nurture it.

One significant effort to reevaluate Transcendence has been made by Dr. R. D. Laing, a psychoanalyst at the Tavistock Clinic in London. In treating psychotic patients evidencing extreme ego loss, Dr. Laing discovered that many such patients were undergoing experiences similar to those described by mystics for centuries. He found that these psychotic breaks were guided by a "will towards health" and, if allowed to run their natural course, led to a positive reintegration in which patients attained great personal insight and improved functioning. Dr. Laing began to treat these psychoses as "voyages of discovery," and established "blow-out centers" in England where they could be experienced in a supportive and warm environment.

His findings have since been supported by the independent research of two Americans, Dr. Julian Silverman a psychologist at the National Institute of Mental Health in Bethesda, Maryland, and Dr. John Weir Perry of the University of California Medical Center in San Francisco. Dr. Silverman has found that certain acute, nonparanoid schizophrenic breaks lead to spontaneous recovery with a measurable increase in the patient's functioning. Dr. Perry has similarly observed that a certain type of schizophrenia follows a course in which patients experience a common train of cosmic religious imagery and "emerge from their psychoses as deeper and broader personalities." Similar findings by the psychiatrist Dr. Kazinierz Dabrowski and his colleagues in Warsaw have been described in Dabrowski's book *Positive Disintegration*. Still another study of the healthful, often transcendent, aspects of psychosis is Anton Boisen's *The Exploration of the Inner World*.

These studies all seem to indicate therefore, that certain forms of what is commonly called "madness" in our society are actually breaks from ordinary consciousness which lead to richer perception and fuller functioning. This new finding is explored by Dr. Laing in his book, *The Politics of Experience*. He writes:

Most people most of the time experience themselves and others in one or another way that I shall call egoic. That is, centrally or peripherally, they experience the world and themselves in terms of a constant identity within a framework of certain ground structures of space and time shared by other members of their society.

However, religious . . . philosophies have agreed that such egoic experience is a preliminary illusion, a veil, a film of maya—a dream to Heraclitus and to Lao Tze, the fundamental illusion of all Buddhism, a state of sleep, of death, of socially accepted madness, a womb state to which one has to die, from which one has to be born. The person going through ego-loss or transcendental experiences may or may not become in different ways confused. Then he might legitimately be regarded as mad. But to be mad is not necessarily to be ill, notwithstanding the fact that in our culture the two categories have become confused. The "ego" is the instrument for living in this world. If the ego is broken up or destroyed (by the insurmountable contradictions of certain life situations, by toxins, chemicals, etc.) then the person may be exposed to other worlds, "real" in different ways from the more familiar territory of dreams, imagination, perception or fantasy.

True sanity entails in one way or another the dissolution of the normal ego, that false self competently adjusted to our alienated social reality; the emergence of the "inner" archetypal mediators of divine power, and through this death a rebirth, and the eventual reestablishment of a new kind of ego functioning, the ego now being the servant of the divine, no longer its betrayer.[5]

While Dr. Laing draws his conclusions from his experience with psychotic patients, contemporary studies of normal human beings indicate that the experience of Transcendence is both a common phenomenon and an important factor in human learning. Abraham Maslow has advanced a theory of man's "inner" nature and the value of transcendental experience which derives from studies of healthy, well-functioning people. As Professor Maslow describes it, man's inner nature seems not to be intrinsically evil, but either neutral or positively "good." Although this inner nature "is weak and delicate and subtle and easily overcome by habit, cultural pressures and wrong attitudes towards it," it consistently works towards fulfillment and makes any therapy or spontaneous recovery possible. In healthy persons, it constantly strives towards realization, or "self-actualization." Personal growth is catalyzed and illuminated by the "peak experiences" of life. These peak experiences are:

> felt as self-validating, self-justifying moments. There is a very characteristic disorientation in time and space. Perception is richer and tends strongly to be idiographic and non-classificatory. The experience, or object, tends to be seen as a whole, as a complete unit, detached from relations, from possible usefulness, from expediency and from purpose . . . many dichotomies, polarities and conflicts are fused, transcended or resolved.

> Cognition during the peak experience is much more passive and receptive than active. The emotional reaction in the peak experience has a special flavor of wonder, of awe, of reverence, of humility and surrender before something great. Perception can be relatively ego-transcending, self-forgetful.

Peak experiences are seemingly egoless, beyond time and space, good and evil. They involve a giving up of self to receive inspiration and knowledge. Furthermore, Professor Maslow notes, they are intense identity experiences in which the creator becomes one with the work being created, just as the mother feels at one with her child. Attainment of integration, identity, autonomy, or selfhood is simultaneously a transcending of the ordinary sense of self.

In a recent study, Marghanita Laski found that the triggers that set off transcendent ecstasy in people from all walks of life include natural scenery, sexual love, childbirth, movement, religion, art, scientific or poetical knowledge, creative work, introspection, and beauty.[6] Like Dr. Laing, who links the experience of his patients with certain precipitate life situations, Mrs. Laski notes that "encounter with a trigger is almost always a necessary precondition for ecstacy, except where ecstatic states are deliberately induced by drugs or disciplines."

Of the disciplines to which Mrs. Laski refers, perhaps the most widely used is meditation, a mental exercise in which attention is focused on an object image or bodily process. The practitioner may be trained to watch rather than direct his thoughts, or to concentrate on an intellectually unsolvable paradox, as in the training of Rinzai Zen. Through this activity, his attention bypasses ordinary cognitive functioning. He becomes a passive witness of his own consciousness, then identifies with and becomes the true self, the source of consciousness.

In spite of its long history in Eastern societies, meditation has remained outside the interest of Western science until recent years, when psychologists began to examine the technique for its relation to the alteration of consciousness.[7] Perhaps the most important innovation derived from this research has been achieved by Dr. Joe Kamiya of the Langley Porter Neuropsychiatric Institute in San Francisco. A research psychologist who has devoted much of his professional life to the study of dreaming, Dr. Kamiya has recently developed a method of training people to control their brain activity. His approach combines methods from experimental psychology, computer technology, and physiology. He feeds back electroencephalographic (EEG) information (brain waves) to trainees in the form of sound and light patterns so that they can hear and see the course of their own brain activity and discover for themselves how to change the sounds and lights by varying their moods and feelings.

Dr. Kamiya first used this technique to train people to discern the alpha functions of their brains. Concurrently, the Japanese researchers Katsamatsu and Hirai discovered that a high, steady rate of alpha waves characterized the EEG records of Japanese Zen masters. Dr. Kamiya has since trained experienced meditators and has found that they can learn to control their alpha functions more readily than trainees selected at random. It is possible that he has accidentally hit upon a crucial index of successful meditation. His work to date suggests that he has found a way to lead people swiftly toward a state of brain activity achieved only after long years of practice.

Since the high alpha state is characterized as being serene and alert, Dr. Kamiya believes the initial application for his technique may be in alleviating human anxiety. But its broadest application may lie in the field of education. As he puts it:

> Education for both young and old has for perhaps too long focused on knowledge about the material and social world outside the learner, or on trained skills where externally observable performances are available. Little systematic effort appears to be devoted to the training of self discernment and self control of the more covert processes of mental activity. For example, events such as after-images, subjective color, heart beats, pains, thoughts, dreams, proprioceptive sensations, day dreams, visual illusions, etc. are not standard curriculum items in the early education of the child, even though they may constitute a substantial portion of the total range of his everyday experience.
>
> In this age of technological sophistication, there seems to be no good reason why a beginning cannot be made toward courses in "physiological awareness," in which students are taught the subjective feel of changes in heart rate, blood pressure, EEG waves, sleep stages, electrodermal changes accompanying social stimuli, gastric contractions, etc.
>
> The dictum "Know Thyself" could be made easier to follow with techniques that make the covert internal processes of brain and body directly observable to the person. . . . When new methods of experiencing the world or self arise, they are eagerly tried. The response of people upon hearing of our laboratory experiments has been almost uniformly "Can I be a subject?" If the research continues to provide further evidence of the relationship between the experiential and the physiological, it is possible that a whole new method of exploring, modifying, and enriching our lives will emerge.

While Dr. Kamiya's method and traditional meditation seek Transcendence in rather solitary circumstances, several modern techniques do so within a group setting. One such technique is the T-group or encounter group developed by psychologists during the past twenty years. This approach is an unstructured stress session, usually lasting twenty-four hours or longer, in which a small number of participants, often strangers at the outset, discuss and develop their feelings towards themselves and one another in a here-and-now setting. The group normally forbids excessive intellectualization and serves as a laboratory in which participants are encouraged to experience previously unfamiliar feelings, to attempt new patterns in their interpersonal relationships, and to attain new insights about themselves and their relations to others. As trust and support develop, once-resisted feelings and perceptions often break through in this deliberately constructed situation. The participants often describe such breakthroughs in specifically religious terms.[8]

The encounter group has been modified by many psychologists in recent years and several professional group leaders have integrated new techniques into the basic group format. Many of these techniques are exercises in physical sensitivity. Dr. William Schutz, for example, a psychologist at the Esalen Institute, has combined elements of fantasy training, psychodrama, and body movement in his workshops, and has led many group participants through personally revealing, often ecstatic experiences.

One such experience was recently reported in the *New York Times Magazine* by San Francisco novelist Leo Litwak, who took part in one of Dr. Schutz's workshops at Big Sur. During the workshop, Litwak became aware that he had closed himself to certain feelings because of overwhelming wartime experiences. He asked Dr. Schutz to lead him on a fantasy excursion through his own body to locate the sources of his emotional coldness. As Litwak describes it,

The trip through my body lasted more than one hour. I found wounds everywhere. I remembered a wounded friend whimpering: — "Help me, Leo," which I did—a close friend, yet after he was hit no friend at all, not missed a second after I heard of his death, numb to him as I was to everyone else, preparing for losses by anesthetizing myself. And in the course of that trip through my body I started to feel again and discovered what I'd missed. I felt wide open, lightened, ready to meet others simply and directly.

Gestalt therapy, a pioneering form of existential psychotherapy, is practiced at Esalen Institute by psychiatrist Dr. Frederick Perls and his students. Dr. Perls believes that men stop growing, or expanding their consciousnesses, because of certain "catastrophic expectations" that chain them to a repetitious status quo. His technique is designed to help people transcend their "impasse points," or limited self-boundaries.

In his workshops, Dr. Perls works with participants individually in a group setting that stimulates feeling and feedback. Participants present him with dreams, fantasies, or feelings; he then asks them to play the several parts of their material or to act out dialogues between the parts. These parts, Dr. Perls believes, are unintegrated facets of personality that must be unified if true growth is to occur. As a participant gets further and further into these dialogues, he reaches an impasse point and flounders helplessly, actually and figuratively afraid to move. Using various techniques, such as shifting the participant's awareness from within to without his body, Dr. Perls tries to lead him through the impasse, freeing suppressed energies and establishing extended boundaries for awareness and behavior. When Dr. Perls is successful, participants often experience rushes of ecstatic feeling, gaining new insight and a sense of integration.

Dr. Perls believes that man's intellect often interferes with the vitality of his physical existence and, "like a computer, deprives us of the vivid immediacy of sensing and experiencing." He emphasizes the inseparability of mind and body and considers his technique a method whereby people can bypass intellectual defenses and free the wisdom of the body. His belief in the body's wisdom is shared by Dr. Alexander Lowen, a New York psychiatrist who has developed several physical exercises to remove obstacles that prevent the body from spontaneously releasing its tensions and thereby "curing itself." Like Dr. Perls, Dr. Lowen has based many of his techniques on the findings of Dr. Wilhelm Reich, a psychiatrist who first identified "character armor" in pathology. This armor includes physical musculature that people develop at an early age to hold back excitation and strong feeling. It serves the ego in denying feelings or unwanted wishes, but at the same time it cripples or desensitizes the body, preventing spontaneous emotion and the possibility of transcendent experience.

In his practice, Lowen combines his physical exercises with verbal therapy. In one such exercise, he has his patients arch their backs over a stool, stretching their back muscles and releasing tensions of the diaphragm. In another, they strike a couch with tennis rackets or kick their legs on a bed to activate pent-up anger. To develop a greater sense of identity, they may tighten the backs of their necks, thrust their jaws forward, and repeat the words "no" and "yes" until they invest more feeling in their articulation. Such techniques allow people to regain their "infantile" capacity of expression, helping them to experience their muscular and personality rigidity. Once such rigidity is known, they may break through the character armor that has stifled their full self-awareness. Once the armor is deeply felt, previously unknown or forgotten truths may become conscious, and the body is freed to effect its own cure.

Dr. Lowen links the high incidence of character armor and chronic tension in our society with our insistence on emotional control in place of healthy spontaneity. In *The Betrayal of the Body* he argues that "civilization" is itself the cause of civilized man's problems:

> . . . the acquisition of knowledge transformed the primitive view of reality. Civilized man discarded the idea of the supernatural; he overcame the awe with which the primitive viewed the unknown and, therefore, mysterious processes of the body and nature; and he replaced the primitive belief in spirits by a faith in the mind and reason. Through its identification with the mind, the ego proclaimed its domination over the body. "I think, therefore I am." Finally, man became egoistic, objective, and detached and lost the feeling of unity with nature.
>
> As long as the ego dominates the individual, he cannot have the oceanic or transcendental experiences that make life meaningful. Since the ego recognizes only direct causes, it cannot admit the

existence of forces beyond its comprehension. Thus, not until the ego bows down to a higher power (as in prayer, for instance) can the individual have a truly religious experience. Not until the ego surrenders to the body in sex can a person have an orgastic experience. And only when the ego abdicates before the majesty of nature will a person have a mystical experience.

It is not my intention to attack the ego or negate the value of knowledge. My argument is that an ego dissociated from the body is weak and vulnerable, and that knowledge divorced from feeling is empty and meaningless. An education that is to be effective in preparing a child for life must take into account his emotional as well as mental development. The school should recognize that spontaneity and pleasure are as important as productivity and achievement.[9]

In spite of this strong criticism from Dr. Lowen and many other psychologists, few schools in America today concern themselves with a child's emotional development. Although the techniques described in the previous pages are being explored at such institutions as the Esalen Institute, the National Training Laboratories, and the Western Behavioral Sciences Institute at La Jolla, California, they have certainly not been integrated into our society. Such integration can only occur when they are included in the curricula of our schools.

The beginnings of such integration are now occurring on some American college campuses. Dr. Schutz and Dr. Perls and several Esalen resident fellows are leading encounter groups, gestalt therapy workshops and other sensitivity training programs at campuses in the San Francisco Bay area and elsewhere. At Stanford University, for example, over one thousand students and faculty members have participated in Esalen's activities.

Similar advances are also being made on the elementary and secondary school level. Educators are increasingly aware that life's important lessons are learned early in a child's development, and many teachers are trying to reach children with sensitivity training before their creativity and spontaneity are stifled entirely in the classroom. A pilot program for this new direction in education was launched by the Esalen Institute last year with the financial assistance of the Ford Foundation. This project is led by Dr. George Brown, professor of education at the University of California at Santa Barbara. Professor Brown is training elementary and secondary school teachers in several techniques derived from or related to those described here, and the teachers themselves are experimenting with them in the classroom. Another similar project in affective education is being conducted in the Philadelphia school system by Terry Borton, Norman Newberg, and others. At Stanford, techniques that trigger transcendent experience have been integrated into regular courses such as design, physical education, and business administration. Similar techniques could enhance the teaching of the arts, philosophy, and psychology.

As the introduction of these techniques into education progresses, it becomes possible to envision a future in which transcendent disciplines for individuals, families, and groups serve as integral facets of Western culture. If, as many futurists predict, affluence and leisure increase and education becomes the raison d'être for most of our lives, the age-old quest for meaning will be forced upon us with new intensity. More than ever, we will need an education to match our hunger for Transcendence.

REFERENCES

1. Many group dynamics programs, in industry and elsewhere, are vehicles for religious joy, though the joy usually goes unnamed in the formal descriptions of these programs. For an exception see James V. Clark, "Toward a Theory and Practice of Religious Experiencing," in James Bugental, ed., *Challenges of Humanistic Psychology* (New York: McGraw-Hill, 1967).
2. Examples of such tradition-oriented groups with substantial followings are the Zen Center of San Francisco, the Transcendental Meditation Society of Mahesh Maharishi, the Krishna Consciousness Society of Swami Bhaktivedanta, and the various groups which have formed around the teachings of Sri Meher Baba, Gurdjieff, and Ouspenski. The Transcendental Meditation Society claims to have more than 10,000 members in the United States.
3. Stanford: Stanford University Press, 1967.
4. One reason perhaps for the wide usage of such terms as "personal growth" and "self-actualization" is their open-endedness and their freedom from the limiting connotations of older terms such as "spiritual development" or "mystical perfection."
5. R. D. Laing, *The Politics of Experience* (New York: Pantheon Books, 1967).

6. Marghanita Laski, *Ecstasy, a Study of Some Secular and Religious Experiences* (Bloomington: Indiana University Press, 1961).

7. See Arthur Deikman's "Experimental Meditation" and "Studies of Meditation" in the *Journal of Nervous and Mental Diseases,* and "De-automatization and the Mystic Experience" in *Pyschiatry.*

8. See "What People in Groups Say," in James Bugental, *op. cit.,* p. 253.

9. New York: Macmillan, 1967, pp. 287–292.

MANIFESTO FOR A DIONYSIAN THEOLOGY

SAM KEEN

I would believe only in a god who could dance.
Nietzsche.

PHILOSOPHERS HOLDING TENURE, theologians committed to the preservation of orthodoxy, intellectuals captivated by ideas, and citizens dedicated to establishing a perimeter of defense against insecurity are reluctant to yield to the rhythm-induced ecstasy of the dance. It is understandable, therefore, that the strange music coming from the wilderness far removed from the academy and the marketplace has not been noted with acclaim in professional journals or the popular press. But the music will go on, for Dionysus is again issuing an invitation to the dance, to ecstasy, enthusiasm, and a touch of divine madness.

Middle-class wisdom looks to Apollo, demands sanity, and accurately maintains that it is dangerous to heed the intoxicating call of Dionysus. Culture depends upon discipline and order; civilization requires civility; even creativity involves sublimation and repression—all of which Dionysus tempts us to forget. In fact, both Dionysian and Apollonian elements are found in any culture, past or present; both chaos and order, ecstasy and discipline are woven into the fabric of all life. Most cultures provide for periodic return through game, festival, and orgy to the chaos that underlies the veneer of civilization (Saturnalia, Mardi Gras) while maintaining the legal order and the social discipline necessary for daily life.

Yet chaos must be domesticated for human community to be possible; the city must build its walls of stone to defend itself against the barbarians without and its structures of law to protect itself from the chaotic passions of its own citizens; the ego must erect

31

defenses against the insistent arational demands of the id. But if order must prevail over chaos, chaos must also have its rights or else vitality is killed by restraint, spontaneity falls prey to the necessity to do everything "decently and in order" (one of the higher laws of Presbyterians), and laughter fades before the spirit of seriousness. When Dionysus is not given his due, Apollo becomes a tyrant, a god to be killed.

Western culture has become increasingly Apollonian and the time has come when the rights of Dionysus must be reasserted. This tyranny of Apollo is especially evident in Western theology and religious institutions, which have for the most part identified with the status quo and been fearful of the chaos of psychological and political revolution. The religious establishment has put its weight behind maintaining the present boundaries, the present forms of personality and social organization. It has counseled that the impulses of the id must either find satisfaction within the existing structures of marriage and society or be repressed, and likewise that political revolution (from the left at any rate) must conform to the rules of capitalism and parliamentary procedure.

If we could once pretend that an Apollonian theology was adequate we no longer can. Both the social revolutions in the underdeveloped countries and the encounter with depth psychology have given irrefutable evidence that the repression of the "lower" classes and the "lower" passions leads only to social and personal sickness. The only way toward health is in learning to live creatively with the chaos within. An integral society, like an integral personality, is the product of a democratic organization within which opposites may coexist in mutual creative interaction. Pluralism is the condition of authentic life, and hence the quest for wholeness, for social and individual healing (salvation), must involve our learning again to praise Dionysus. For when Dionysus is denied the honor due him, the healing power of reformation, ecstasy, wonder, and grace is lost.

From the fringes of contemporary thought is coming a renewed vision of Dionysian way of life. While it would be too much to claim that there is a self-conscious school of Dionysian thinkers, Thomas Altizer, Norman O. Brown, Nikos Kazantzakis, Herbert Marcuse, and Alan Watts are all centrally concerned with themes which can fairly be called Dionysian, as in a lesser degree are Heidegger, Marcel, Tillich, and Whitehead. This essay will trace in broad outline the worldview and life style of the Dionysian way with special reference to theology. We will first contrast the Apollonian and the Dionysian ways and, after suggesting a corrective in the Dionysian understanding of the self, will advocate the necessity of recovering the Dionysian element in theology. Our concern is to discover what it might be like if we had the courage and/or folly to accept the invitation to dance our way through life.

THE APOLLONIAN WAY

Apollo is the god who most fully incarnates the ideals we associate with classical Greek thought. He is the god of the ego, of light, youth, purity, reasonableness, order, discipline, and balance. Perhaps the most characteristic maxim of the Apollonian way is the one that Socrates adopted from the oracle at Delphi as the basis of a philosophy of life—"Know thyself!" Know thyself to be a man, to be limited in time and space; above all do not commit the folly of *hubris,* do not in pride presume to exceed the limits of mortality and aspire to the conditions of the gods.

Wisdom, in the Apollonian tradition, consists of learning the rules and boundaries and in distinguishing with clarity between that which belongs to mortality and that which is immortal, between the knowable and the unknowable, the possible and the impossible, man and God, I and thou, mine and yours. The happy man, having learned the proper limits of humanity, follows the way of moderation and seeks to govern the rebellious forces of the senses and the wayward imagination by the imposition of discipline. The psyche of man is a commonwealth which the wise man will subject to the rule of reason. One might well see in Plato's figure of the Demiurge one model for the Apollonian view of man.

Like the architect of the universe, man also must be a craftsman, a fabricator (*homo faber*) who grasps the ideal of reason and by force of will imposes it upon the recalcitrant and chaotic givenness of life. Man shares with the gods the responsibility for creating a cosmos in which reason and order prevail. The rule of law is the path of wisdom. Man must distinguish between the good and the evil, the permissible and the impermissible; and then, as a citizen in a commonwealth under law, must take the responsibility for tailoring his inner and outer life to conform to what is required, to the laws governing nature, society, the psyche, and the relationship between God and man. Whatever impulses, desires, or actions run counter to the order necessary to a harmonious commonwealth must be repressed.

The Apollonian way has come to dominate Western culture. Science and technology rest upon distinguishing, clarifying, and gaining controlling knowledge over the environment. The world of science is the realm of law and regularity where personal desires and impulses are disciplined and brought into conformity to the objective and verifiable modes of thought of the scientific community. Western political and psychological organization also tends to stress private property, individual responsibility, and the unique identity of the individual. We have come to see man as an atom living in a society of atoms cut off both from the natural order below and the "super-natural" order above.

The Apollonian organization of modern life is visible as one flies across the United States or any Western country. Where man is, order is obvious. The geometric patterns which we impose on our fields and cities reveal our passion for neat boundaries, for the discipline of ownership, for distinguishing between my possessions and yours. Our laws which stress individual responsibility and guilt show that we organize psychic space in the same way we structure physical space. Guilt before the law implies that one is in *full possession* of the personal faculties which make for responsibility.

The dominance of the Apollonian way has been especially evident in theology. Western theology has always been strongly theistic in its doctrine of God. God is *a* being, transcendent and separate from his creation; he must not be confused with the world or with any part of the world. Both Kierkegaard and Barth are typically Apollonian in their insistence that we must recognize "an absolute qualitative distinction between time and eternity," between man and God. God must keep his boundaries sacrosanct, and the theologian as the explicator of his revelation must be jealous to destroy any theology which suggests that anything finite can mingle with God. Pantheism and mysticism are theologically suspect, as both Niebuhr and Brunner have argued, because they teach an unseemly confusion of God and the natural order, either as God becomes wholly incarnate in the world in pantheism, or as man finds a point of identity with God in his own soul in mysticism.

The Apollonian God is a jealous God. Those who would trespass on his omnipotent and transcendent glory must be reminded that "good fences make good neighbors." God alone can overcome the distance between himself and everything finite, and because he is a God of love he has chosen to leave his isolation and reveal himself to man in special places and times. In certain "mighty acts," such as the exodus of the Israelites from Egypt and the life, death, and resurrection of Jesus, God has chosen to be Emmanuel (God with us), to overcome the distance that otherwise separates the creatures from the Creator. The traditional theistic understanding of God's revelation in special acts, events, and persons has created a dichotomy between the sacred and the profane and has led to the segregation of the experience of the holy from the realm of the everyday.

One other aspect of a dominantly Apollonian theology must be noted. Nietzsche, Sartre, Altizer, and others have charged that an Apollonian concept of a creator God is necessarily repressive of human dignity and freedom. The God of theism is a creator who fabricates the world out of nothing through the instrument of his reason (*logos*). Like a good craftsman, God gives the world order, structure, rationality, and law. Man as a creature can find authentic life only by discovering God's plan for his life, only by actualizing the essence which he was potentially given in creation, only by obedience to the "will" of God.

Thus the creator God becomes the omniscient judge who rewards and punishes those who obey and those who rebel against the standards which he has programmed into his created order. As the one who oversees the whole course of history, God is the critical audience before whom the drama of life is played. (Billy Graham: "Remember when you read those sexy magazines—God is watching you.") Such a God may be merciful and forgiving, the eye which watches may be kindly, but he is responsible for the "oughts," he is the definer of what human life should be. Man is authentic in obedience, not in self-creation. Increasingly modern man has felt that he must rebel against such a God and assert his right to be for himself, to create his own oughts, to define for himself the nature of good and evil. This rebellion has been carried on with the help of Dionysus, to whom we now turn.

THE DIONYSIAN WAY

Dionysus was a strange and wild god, an import both to the Greek countryside and the Greek spirit. He seems to have originated in Thrace, where he was a god of fertility and the energy of nature. On Greek soil he became associated with wine as well as with the metamorphosis which is symbolized in the cycle of the seasons. The worship of Dionysus was literally enthusiastic; it involved ecstasy, license, revelry, and direct participation by eating in the life of the dying and reborn god. In the ecstasy induced by wine and dancing the worshipers lost their own personalities and were merged with Dionysus. Thus the boundaries separating man, nature, and the divine were erased.

The essence of the Dionysian way is that it dares the extreme and hence leads to a form of consciousness which is alien to the law-abiding and mean-regarding character of the Apollonian mind. The Dionysian way exalts ecstasy over order, the id over the ego, being possessed over a possessive orientation, the creative chaos of freedom over the security of inherited patterns of social and psychological organization, and divine madness over repressed sanity. As Nietzsche pointed out in his study of the Apollonian and Dionysian types, it is Prometheus who is the model of the Dionysian way. Prometheus transgressed the boundaries of *hubris* in stealing the fire from the gods and was, therefore, condemned to punishment. The hard lesson he teaches is: "Man's highest good must be bought with a crime and paid for by the flood of grief and suffering which the offended divinities visit upon the human race in its noble ambition." [1]

Both the Genesis myth and Freud's mythology teach the same

lesson: man becomes man only by breaking the laws which would refuse him the personal knowledge of good and evil, only by "killing the father," the source of authority and power, who would keep him forever in a state of childhood and dependence. Only in abolishing the "law," in denying any authority that dictates what he must become, does man become free.

Wisdom in the Dionysian tradition consists of continuing openness to the diverse and sometimes contradictory streams that flow through the depths of man. Man is not a property whose boundaries must be guarded against the intrusion of chaos by the watchful eye of the ego and its symbolically masked agents, but it is a nexus (Whitehead), a field of awareness where all dimensions of reality converge. The boundaries are created by the possessive instinct, by the cultural ideologies which sacrifice vividness to security and ecstasy to order. In yielding to possession by the god, one is inhabited by a holy power that informs all life, and the boundaries are broken down between I and thou, man and nature, man and God, ego and id.

The self exists by its mystical participation in the power of being, which is in all things. Once the boundaries of the ego are broken down, the self is understood not so much as a substance that has its own resident source of power but as one focus of a universal power, taking, for the moment, the form of an individual man. Nietzsche has spoken of the Dionysian way as one in which the principle of individuation is lost:

> Not only does the bond between man and man come to be forged once more by the magic of the Dionysiac rite, but nature itself, long alienated or subjugated, rises again to celebrate the reconciliation with her prodigal son, man. The earth offers its gifts voluntarily, and the savage beasts of the mountain and desert approach in peace. . . . Now the slave emerges as a freeman; all the rigid, hostile walls which either necessity or despotism has erected between men are shattered. Now that the gospel of universal harmony is sounded, each individual becomes not only reconciled to his fellow but actually at one with him—as though the veil of Maya had been torn apart and there remained only shreds floating before the vision

of mystical Oneness. Man now expresses himself through song and dance as the member of a higher community; he has forgotten how to walk, how to speak, and is on the brink of taking wings as he dances. Each of his gestures betokens enchantment; through him sounds a supernatural power, the same power which makes the animals speak and the earth render up milk and honey. He feels himself to be godlike and strides with the same elation and ecstasy as the gods he has seen in his dreams. No longer the *artist*, he has himself become *a work of art;* the productive power of the whole universe is now manifest in his transport, to the glorious satisfaction of the primordial One. . . .[2]

This loss of individuality, which is at the heart of the Dionysian way, has been expressed by modern thinkers in diverse terminology. Heidegger makes a complete analysis of the human condition without using the word "man." Man becomes *dasein*, "being there," an instance of Being, not a hermetic substance with an autonomous power of being. Norman O. Brown understands authentic life as requiring the death of the ego and a passivity by which *we are lived,* inhabited.

The *id* is instinct; that Dionysian "cauldron of seething excitement," a sea of energy out of which the ego emerges like an island. The term *"id"*—"it"—taken from Nietzsche (via Groddeck), is based on the intuition that the conduct through life of what we call our ego is essentially passive; it is not so much we who live as that we are lived, by unknown forces. The reality is instinct, and instinct is impersonal energy, an "it" who lives in us. I live, yet not I, but it lives in me; as in creation, *fiat.* Let it be; no "I" but an it. The "I–Thou" relationship is still a relation to Satan; the old Adversary; the Accuser; to whom we are responsible; or old Nobodaddy in the garden, calling Adam, where art thou? Let there be no one to answer to.[3]

Alan Watts, drawing on the insights of Zen and Eastern mysticism, makes substantially the same point as Brown. The authentic life, which Buddhism has spoken of as *nirvana,* involves losing the illusion of the ego as a separate agent.

Nirvana is a radical transformation of how it feels to be alive: it feels as if everything were myself, or as if everything—including "my" thoughts and actions—were happening of itself. There are still efforts, choices, and decisions, but not in the sense that "I *make* them"; they arise of themselves in relation to circumstances.[4]

If the more characteristic models for the Apollonian way are the activities of fabrication (God making the world in conformity with his *Logos,* man making himself in the image of some ideal) and legislation (God and man projecting laws which hold chaos in check and allow community), the model for the Dionysian way is the dance. Life is flux, movement, a dynamic power which assumes form for a moment and then changes. There is no end-point, no complete product. In the strict sense of the word there can be no integrity (a state of being complete, whole, unbroken) of individual life. Everything is a fraction, incomplete without its counterpart.

In the dance of life, male and female, work and play, creativity and fallowness, day and night, life and death belong together in a *rhythmic* unity. Identity is in movement, in the economy of fractions which create a community in diversity. Authentic thought is, as Nietzsche said, thought which dances. Kazantzakis' figure of Zorba the Greek might well be taken as a concrete illustration of the Dionysian way and of the centrality of dance as an organizing metaphor for life. Zorba dances when the joy or the tragedy of life overflows the capacity of his words.

Two other metaphors are also frequently used to characterize the Dionysian way: fire and war. Fire, like a dance, is always moving and consuming what it touches; life is not being but becoming, not substance but process, as Heraclitus said at the beginning of Western philosophy and as Hegel and Whitehead have reminded us more recently. Fire and dance are also war, because in the flux of experience the opposites belong together. Life is dialectic, hence thesis and antithesis are bound together in conflict. True warfare, like dance, like sex, like contest *(agon)*, requires friendly enemies, requires the love of the enemy. Human communication at its best is, as Jaspers has said, "loving combat." We wrestle together in dialogue (which is polite warfare) in order that the whole truth may emerge from the incomplete and fractured individual perspectives.

The Dionysian way is one of iconoclasm or of what might be called "muraloclasm" (breaking down the walls). In destroying the traditional boundaries and limits that inform our accepted notions of personality and society, the Dionysian way flirts with madness. As psychoanalysis has demonstrated, there is at the depths of every person a wilderness, a chaos never domesticated by the "identity" we assume or the "personality" we put on "to meet the faces that we meet." The Dionysian wisdom is that we must immerse ourselves in this wilderness, which we usually repress and know only in dreams, daydreams (both brief psychotic episodes), and in the cultivated symbols of art and religion. The source of the power for vivid life lies locked in the unconscious. To be vital we must risk madness, as Zorba the Greek points out in his criticism of the life style of his Apollonian "Boss."

> "No, you're not free," he said. "The string you're tied to is perhaps longer than other people's. That's all. You're on a longer piece of string, boss; you come and go, and think you're free, but you never cut the string in two. It's difficult, boss, very difficult. You need a touch of folly to do that; folly, d'you see? You have to risk everything! But you've got such a strong head, it'll always get the better of you. A man's head is like a grocer; it keeps accounts: I've paid so much and earned so much and that means a profit of this much or a loss of that much! The head's a careful little shopkeeper; it never risks all it has, always keeps something in reserve. It never breaks the string. Ah no! It hangs on tight to it, the bastard! If the string slips out of its grasp, the head, poor devil, is lost, finished! But if a man doesn't break the string, tell me what flavor is left in life? The flavor of camomile, weak camomile tea. Nothing like rum—that makes you see life inside out![5]

Norman Brown gives the same speech as Zorba, changing only the rhetoric:

> Dionysus, the mad god, breaks down the boundaries; releases the prisoners; abolishes repression; and abolishes the *principium indivi-duationis,* substituting for it the unity of man and the unity of man with nature. In this age of schizophrenia, with the atom, the individual self, the boundaries disintegrating, there is, for those who would save our souls, the ego-psychologists, "The Problem of Iden-

tity." But the breakdown is to be made into a breakthrough; as Conrad said, in the destructive element immerse. The soul that we call our own is not a real one. The solution to the problem of identity is, get lost. Or as it says in the New Testament: "He that findeth his own psyche shall lose it, and he that loseth his psyche for my sake shall find it."[6]

We are here at the heart of the Dionysian view of man. And a problematic heart it is! If the boundaries established by the ego are to be broken down in order that direct participation in the divine power which pervades all may be experienced, what of the self who remains the focus of experience? The Dionysian way has never been able to offer an adequate doctrine of the person. Norman Brown and Alan Watts both make frequent use of the Buddhist idea of no-self. Once the self strips off those items of its identity which are accumulated from the repressive demands of parents and culture, from the defense mechanisms which insist upon uniqueness and separateness, there is no ego left, no unique identity which distinguishes one man from another.

Our illusions of uniqueness and separateness arise out of our internalization of masks (personalities) and models. Our ego is a theater, and it is the masks we wear and the roles we feel compelled to play that separate us. Once the masks drop and the performance before the audience of the introjected parental figures—and others from whom approval is necessary—ceases, there is no more ego, no more internal theater, no defense mechanisms. There remains only a perceiving mind that now realizes its oneness with all things.

By way of criticism we must insist that while it is evident from the therapeutic success of the psychoanalytic method that psychic health demands openness to the unconscious, to the repressed awareness of the totality of experience, it is equally evident that some principle of identity or selfhood is necessary for authentic and vivid life. When Norman Brown advocates schizophrenia as the divine madness appropriate to the Dionysian way of life, he ignores a crucial distinction between garden variety insanity and that divine madness which is the essence of creativity and joy. There is a vast difference between a schizophrenic who has no ego strong enough to screen the chaotic intrusions from the unconscious, and hence is submerged in a state of chaos in which there is neither clarity nor joy, and the person who has learned to be open to the depths of emotion and feeling and to the whole range of symbolism which lies beneath the surface of daily preoccupations. The schizophrenic has no person; he is lacking in the unity and the sense of limits which are necessary to even minimal functioning in a social context. The healed schizophrenic, if we may use that term for the Dionysian type of personality organization, is aware of the glory and horror of being human. He knows that the difference between himself and the murderer is only that he dreams what the murderer does, as well as what the saint does. He is aware of the diverse possibilities which exist within himself, of the underworld of hatred and the overworld of dreams and ideals, of the hope and the despair, of the child that remains within. Yet the healed schizophrenic is also in touch with some principle of unity within himself. Call this principle of unity the self, the person, or whatever, but unity there must be if we are to distinguish between that insanity in which there is no transcendence but only tragedy and that divine madness in which the individual knows himself to be a part of that unifying power which binds together the kaleidoscope of reality.

My suggestion is that we call the Dionysian form of consciousness in which there is tolerance of the plurality within the self *inclusive self-consciousness,* as distinguished from the Apollonian *exclusive ego-consciousness* in which the ego is felt as a sensitive enclosure whose boundaries must be protected from all that is alien or strange. Inclusive self-consciousness is, in Marcel's terms, available *(disponible)*; it keeps open house for strange visitors from far and near without being threatened by the new, the unexpected, or the disorienting. The authentic Dionysian consciousness prefers astonishment to possession; wonder is its rule of life, its charter of organization.

The principle of organization that gives unity to the inclusive self-consciousness of the Dionysian person is the rhythmic oscillation between the formation of models or self-images and iconoclasm. The authentic self continually sets boundaries and limits by its introjection of ideals and images of what it is and what it would like to be and then it destroys these boundaries as experience overflows them. Psychological and spiritual health does not consist in having no self but in keeping the process of self-formation flowing, of continually enlarging the images by which we understand ourselves and our world. In this way the Dionysian self is always in process of becoming more open, more wondering, more permissive of that strangeness and novelty which renews the sense of limitless possibilities and increases the capacity to hope. Dionysian man is *homo viator* (Marcel), a pilgrim, a gypsy, a dancer. His security lies in learning to be at home on the road. By contrast Apollonian man is a homesteader who stakes out a territory with defined limits and possibilities and finds his security in the defense of this territory. He lives by what Robert Ardrey called "the territorial imperative."

DIONYSIAN THEOLOGY

Just as the Apollonian way had an appropriate theological expression in traditional Western theism, the Dionysian way also has its characteristic understanding of God, revelation, and the style of the religious life.

The symbol of dance best captures the unique emphasis of a Dionysian theology's idea of God. Nietzsche's statement may serve as a starting point.

> I would believe only in a god who could dance. And when I saw my devil I found him serious, thorough, profound, and solemn: it was the spirit of gravity—through him all things fall.
> Not by wrath does one kill but by laughter. Come, let us kill the spirit of gravity!
> I have learned to walk: ever since, I let myself run.
> I have learned to fly: ever since, I do not want to be pushed before moving along.
> Now I am light, now I fly, now I see myself beneath myself, now a god dances through me.[7]

In order to understand the significance of the symbol of a dancing God we must go back briefly to the Apollonian theological tradition. Western theology, until modern times, has never been free of the Aristotelian concept of God as the Unmoved Mover. God has been a giver, never a receiver, a frigid God to whom no value accrued from the world. Even where Christian theology has spoken of God's death upon the cross, it has never allowed suffering, change, or time to be taken into the life of God himself. When the Apollonian tradition has allowed movement within God it was not because he was understood as being intimately related to the chaotic and tragic flux of time, but because he was trinitarian and thus, being a plenum of perfection and reality, had internal relations between the "persons" of the Godhead.

God's self-sufficient perfection has precluded his passionate involvement in the movement and suffering that is human history. Many theological dodges have been thought up to allow God both the static perfection of his eternal being and the semblance of a relation to time, but always the Apollonian tradition has come out on the side of the perfection, aseity, and impassability of God. As the Methodist discipline reminds us: God is without "body, parts, or passions." That which is perfect cannot change, that which suffers cannot be God; hence God is ultimately beyond change and suffering; he is an unmoved mover; he does not dance; he is substance not process.

Modern theology has increasingly rejected the notion of an unmoved mover, of a God in whom there is "no shadow of change," and has come to speak of a dancing God, a God whose perfection is in process, whose life is involved in the relativities of relationship. A static God is dead. Under the impact of scientific categories which show that all "substance" is process, that mass is energy, that being is relationship, theology has rejected the Apollonian God of defined boundaries and self-sufficient life; the God whose sole activity was knowing himself, whose mode of creation was through the instrumentality of *logos,* whose "ideas" formed the essence of all things. The thinkers associated with this change are many. Other than those we have mentioned as seeking to create a Dionysian theology, process theologians such as Whitehead and Hartshorne have made the most substantial contribution.

A God who is changed and relativized by a real relationship with the moving face of human history is no longer the theistic God of Apollonian theology. A Dionysian theology tends in the direction of pantheism or panentheism. God is not a being but Being itself, or the ground of being. Whether God transcends the world is a moot question (this being the issue between pantheism and panentheism), but the immanence of God is stressed. God is not a strange being enthroned beyond time and space in unchangeable glory who occasionally condescends to invade our planet by means of a mighty act or an incarnation. God is the creative power at the heart of all things. As the Oryxhynchus Papyrus reports Jesus as saying: "Wherever there are two, they are not without God; and where there is one alone I say I am with him. Lift up the stone and there shalt thou find me; cleave the wood, and I am there."

One of the reasons a Dionysian theology finds it necessary to reject the traditional Apollonian concept of a monarchical God isolated in eternity and revealed primarily in an inaccessible past (and these ideas logically involve each other, for it is only a distant God who must occasionally make himself known in an otherwise secular world by way of mighty acts) is that such a theology is inevitably both *repressive* and *regressive*. Before the face of the God who is the Absolute Monarch of the Universe man always stands under scrutiny and judgment. Nietzsche, Sartre, Brown, and Altizer have all stressed the repressive nature of the traditional concept of God. Before the omniscient eye we are reduced to objects who may only obey or rebel; we become artifacts of a Cosmic Artisan devoid of any real freedom to give meaning to our own lives. Life becomes a performance before an all-seeing spectator. As Norman Brown notes, such a transcendent judge is really the projection of the image of the father, the superego ideal made absolute. As long as such an idea of God is held:

> the distinction between public and private disappears; we are on stage at all times. Christianity will not be rid of the performance principle, will not become a pure principle of invisible grace, until it gets rid of the specter of the Father, Old Nobodaddy, the watching institution.[8]

The God who is really for man must genuinely be *with* him, he must leave the boundaries of his own isolation (always a sign of defensive weakness) and incarnate himself in the movement of human history. Altizer, using language that is still Christocentric, finds the unique meaning of Christian theology in its radical incarnational principle. He can go so far as to insist that the old God is dead and therefore the transcendent ground of repression and guilt is broken. Christianity is the good news that the distant and transcendent God who showed himself only in the sacred preserve of some past time is dead.

> The Christian Word appears in neither a primordial nor an eternal form; for it is an incarnate Word, a Word that is real only to the extent that it becomes one with human flesh. If we are to preserve the uniqueness of the Christian Word, we cannot understand the Incarnation as a final and once-and-for-all event of the past. On the contrary, the Incarnation must be conceived as an active and forward-moving process, a process that even now is making all things new. . . .[9]

A Dionysian theology says that a man must lose his life if he is to gain it, that the defensiveness of the ego must give way to inclusive self-consciousness that acknowledges the communion of the self with the whole world, that the rigid boundaries of our "unique" personalities are the product of a possessive and repressive orientation to life. Such a theology cannot worship a God who is understood on the model of that isolated life which in man arises out of weakness and fear. God is God in giving himself, in losing his boundaries, in entering into the dance of history.

If God loses himself in the dance of history the radical question of the appropriateness of retaining "God" language arises. If the boundaries separating God, nature, and man are abolished does it make any sense to continue speaking of God? The Dionysian "God" is not a transcendent object or person to be known by the inbreaking of revelation at certain unique points, but rather the power of "the creative good" (Wieman) or the "power of being" in all things (Tillich). The justification for continuing to speak about God is pragmatic and epistemological. Man must have symbols which grasp and articulate his intuition of what he experiences as ultimate. The symbols are always objectifying but the reality they point to overflows all conceptual boundaries. "God" language functions to focus celebration and adoration on those sacred dimensions of reality which are known in the ecstatic experiences of love, creativity, hope, joy, and thanksgiving.

What is ultimately the case about the whole of reality is beyond human powers of perception. At best man can only yield to those experiences in which he senses the presence of a power which urges human life toward a richer harmony. If he names this power "God" it is because he confesses that the power by which life is sustained and invited toward wholeness is no human creation and abides and remains steadfast even in a world where death does have dominion over every individual. To speak of God is to safeguard man against the pathetic arrogance which presumes to possess this power rather than be possessed by it.

In a Dionysian theology, revelation, which is merely man's awareness of the presence of the holy, is not limited either to special events in some past history of salvation or to any special realm of the sacred. Reality as a whole is sacramental. Any tree, person, or event may become transparent to the holy power that informs every living thing. Revelation is always new; it is a process not a product. The world is the vocabulary of God. In opening ourselves to life as a gift to be enjoyed and utilized with responsibility, we may find that which makes us whole, which undergirds our lives with the certainty of dignity and value at any point in our experience.

A Dionysian view or revelation moves in what Tillich called a radically "theonomous" direction. The ordinary is seen as holy. There are no special times and places, no privileged sections of history. Revelation is homogenized into the quotidian; it is found in the ordinary rather than the *extra*ordinary. Van Gogh's paintings reveal clearly the Dionysian vision of the reality of the everyday permeated with the presence of the holy. In a letter he stated:

> I can very well do without God, both in my life and my painting, but I cannot, ill as I am, do without something which is greater than I, which is my life—the power to create. . . . And in a picture I want to say something comforting as music is comforting. I want to paint men and women with that something of the eternal which the halo used to symbolize, and which we seek to give by the actual radiance and vibration of our colorings.[10]

In the same spirit Norman Brown writes:

Dionysus calls us outdoors. . . . Out of the temple made with hands; out of the ark of the book; out of the cave of the law; out of the belly of the letter. The first tabernacle in Jerusalem; the second tabernacle the universal Church; the third tabernacle the open sky.[11]

The Dionysian way understands theological language as arising out of those experiences which are dense with meaning and value. In love, trust, wonder, hope, and other such experiences having what Marcel called "ontological weight," we find life a holy gift and identify its source as "God." Theological language is a way of giving form to those wondering moments when we find ourselves possessed by a power which makes life whole and holy. The language is merely a handle we use to understand and to maintain ourselves in a condition of openness to this power. As such it must always be a means, an instrument which is abandoned when it ceases to function creatively. A living theology demands a constant process of iconoclasm and renaming of the holy. There are no holy words, not even the word God.

A valid theology constantly orders and extrapolates the implications of the experience of that power of being which gives meaning and value to life. The traditional symbols of theology are not a correct system of language to be memorized but a museum of models or linguistic maps of the way in which the religious intuition has been articulated in the past. Loyalty to the tradition does not mean that we accept the adequacy of past models and maps; only that we learn from them the principles of theological mapmaking. Theological language is a way of handling experiences, of clarifying and orienting ourselves. It is a creation of man and hence it is a human responsibility to make the language function in a way which maximizes the creative potentials of the human community.

To admit that theological language is a projection, a creation of man, is neither to deny that it makes cognitive claims concerning God nor is it to reduce theology to an illusion. It is merely to admit that the sources of all that is, the holy power which we apprehend as the foundation of human dignity and meaning, can only be conceived in human terms, in stories, myths, symbols. The God from whom human life is a gift can never be adequately named, hence we are responsible at a minimum to be flexible in our adherence to symbols for the ultimate, lest our allegiance turn into idolatry and we give our loyalty to symbols which have become repressive.

Theologically as well as psychologically man must remain a pilgrim, a wayfarer; epistemologically and linguistically he is *homo viator.* Recognizing the relativity of all his modes of perceiving and articulating, the religious man must strike his theological tents and move on when the waters of life dry up where there has traditionally been an oasis. Man must give names to the ultimate if he is to possess and understand his experience, but he must be willing to undergo the painful process of iconoclasm and reformation.

Perhaps the real sin against the holy spirit is the refusal to move to new linguistic and institutional forms that keep things verdant when the old names and organizations have become parched and devoid of life. A living theology is a dance, the rhythmic oscillation between the experiences of the nameless power that gives life and invites us to wholeness and the domestication of that power through language and institutions. The same principle which governs the organization of inclusive self-consciousness governs an authentic Dionysian theology—there must be continual reformation of the images and models by which we understand and give shape to our lives.

Apollonian theology, with its assumption that the decisive revelation of God took place in the past, has always been oriented around the *hearing* of the word in which the memory and witness of God's mighty acts is preserved. Tradition, which is the codified memory of the sacred time of the distant God's inbreaking in history, is the instrument of revelation; the ear is the organ of religious perception. By contrast, a Dionysian theology assumes that the decisive revelation of God's presence in history takes place in the present. God is perceived as the source of the gift of life and the power which invites us toward wholeness in every present moment of experience.

Tradition is illustration; the memory of God's acts that is preserved in the literature and discourse of the theological community (the church or synagogue) is important to the present-day believer only to the extent that it helps him interpret *his own personal and social history* as revelatory, as undergirded by that which assures dignity and meaning to human existence. This means that Dionysian theology is oriented toward the *eye*, the senses, and the body. It seeks the fullest possible participation in the present moment; it urges that we taste and see and feel the world, that we penetrate to the abiding dimensions of meaning and value that are within the immediate moment of experience.

In assuming that the present moment is the time of revelation we become involved in a theology of affection and emotion. Our basic feelings of wonder or possession, trust or mistrust, expectation or boredom, hope or despair, nostalgia or satiety, love or fear, potency or impotency are far more fundamental to the way we actually position ourselves in and experience our world than the linguistic systems and ideas that we articulate. A God whose revelation *was* in the flesh but for the contemporary believer primarily *is* in the Word will be absent from the substance of human life and present only in its rationalizations and ideologies. To the degree that our primarily religious perception is a matter of memory, God is dead. If we are unable to identify any power which we may call God in our present feelings and experience then we had best let God language be "antiqued" and preserved for its decorative value.

The God of past mighty acts cannot fill our need for a sanctifying power which makes us whole in the present moment. To isolate God either in transcendence or in past history is to destroy him. Since that is what most western theology has done it is little wonder that the secret has been let out—"God is Dead." Either we learn how to use our theological language to identify the action of God in the dynamics of present experience or we capitulate. The dominant emphasis of contemporary theology on the revelation of the transcendent God in special mighty acts in history is built upon an empty slogan. There is no such thing as history divorced from nature or experience. All theology has arisen from man's effort to interpret the world given to him in experience. "God" and "act of God" are interpretations of experience.

The real question separating Apollonian and Dionysian theologies is "In whose experience is the holy normatively revealed for our time? In our forefathers or our own?" A Dionysian theology proclaims that we must return to basic experiences and attitudes, such as trust, love, wonder, joy, sorrow, hope, and despair, in order that we may learn again how to speak with integrity about what is holy and sacred. It may well be that in recovering a wondering openness to our total experience we may discover that ours is a holy place, that the events of our own personal histories tell a story of promise and fulfillment and give testimony to the presence of a power within human history which makes for wholeness and freedom.

To accept the Dionysian invitation to the dance is not without danger. Revolution is a radical solution. It only remains to consider whether in this time of psychological and political crisis anything less than a radical solution is adequate. Should we by foolishness or courage discover that we may celebrate the holiness of life in any time and place, we might be induced to question that other form of madness which has brought us to the edge of moral and political nihilism—the unquestioned Apollonian assumption that impulse must be repressed and revolution be dealt with by violence, even at the cost of napalmed innocence. If out of timidity or the desire for security we refuse the ecstasy of allowing our ideas, our bodies and our institutions to dance, perhaps there remains only that form of insanity which expends its substance in defending some absolute qualitative distinction between U.S. defense of freedom and communist aggression or in insisting on some 17th parallel dividing time from eternity.

SUMMARY

Without denying that an adequate philosophy or theology will partake of both Apollonian and Dionysian elements, we have maintained that our time is predominantly in need of recovering the Dionysian element. The respective emphases of these two ways may be summarized:

THE APOLLONIAN WAY	THE DIONYSIAN WAY
Man-the-maker, fabricator, molder and manipulator of environment.	Man-the-dancer responding to the givenness of life in its multiplicity.

Domination of the ego, emphasis upon erecting boundaries, giving form, intellectual and material possession. The will and the intellect are central.

Value is created by action. Authentic life is aggressive, "masculine," active.

Domination of the id. Emphasis upon destroying boundaries, exploration of diversity, chaos, vitality. Feeling and sensation are central.

Value is discovered, it is given as we encounter the world in wonder. Authentic life involves passivity, accepting, responding.

As translated into theological idiom the two ways yield an emphasis upon:

Theism or deism. God is *a* being encountered as a Thou, revealing himself in unique acts in history.

A theology of the Word, work, action, speaking, willing, thinking, consciousness, order.

Pantheism or Panentheism. God is being itself, the encompassing, the power of being in all, known in the density of experiences in which value is discovered.

A theology of the spirit, leisure, play, listening, waiting, feeling, chaos, the unconscious.

1. Friedrich Nietzsche, *The Birth of Tragedy* (New York: Doubleday, 1956), p. 64.
2. *Ibid.*, p. 24.
3. Norman O. Brown, *Love's Body* (New York: Random House, 1966), p. 88.
4. Alan Watts, *Psychotherapy East and West* (New York: Mentor Books, 1966), p. 60.
5. Nikos Kazantzakis, *Zorba the Greek* (New York: Simon & Schuster, 1965), p. 300.
6. Brown, *op. cit.*, p. 116.
7. Friedrich Nietzsche, *Thus Spake Zarathustra,* in Walter Kaufmann, *The Portable Nietzsche* (New York: Viking Press, 1954), p. 153.
8. Brown, *op. cit.*, p. 106.
9. Thomas Altizer, *The Gospel of Christian Atheism* (Philadelphia: Westminster Press, 1966), p. 40.
10. Quoted in Herbert Read, *The Meaning of Art* (London: Faber & Faber), p. 206.
11. Brown, *op. cit.*, p. 229.

FEASIBILITY AND FANTASY: SOURCES OF SOCIAL TRANSCENDENCE

HARVEY COX

IN ONE OF HIS ESSAYS Michael Harrington asserts that our society has lost the capacity for utopian fantasy. Our images of the future tend to be drawn as extensions of the present. Our imagination has atrophied. Unlike previous generations whose visions of the society transcended their means of accomplishing them, we suffer from a surplus of means and a shortage of visions. In this sense we have lost the capacity for transcending the present.

I think the evidence bears out Harrington's point. The many-colored maps of urban planners rarely include any ideas which are not quantitative extrapolations from existing cities. Planning institutes project futures which look woefully similar to the present in most of their characteristics. Even in that bedlam of future speculation, science fiction, the asteroid ages depicted seem to be marked mainly by vastly expanded and refined technologies. Space travel, telecommunication, robotry, and weapons systems have all been "improved," but nothing really new has entered the picture. In "Star Trek" the military mentality and the atmosphere of conflict have reached out to encompass the whole solar system and beyond. In *Walden Two* conflict has been eliminated, but people live in a world of controls imposed upon them from without. In *2001* man has still not solved the crises of his relation to his own tools. The problem is that when we run out of images of the future which are radically at variance with what we have now we limit the possible range of changes. We initiate a self-fulfilling prophecy mechanism resulting in more of the same. This process eventually produces social and cultural stagnation, leading to an inert society.

In his historical survey of Western man's way of thinking about the future, *The Image of the Future*, Fred L. Polak argues that the main dynamic in Western history has been contributed by images of the future. He suggests, like Harrington, that our failure to create new future images can result in what he calls "timeless time," a steady state situation in which innovation applies only to means and no longer to ends.[1]

Why has this happened? Why have we lost this particular capacity for self-transcendence? What part can religion play in restoring the capacity for imaginative self-transcendence?

Let me begin my response to these questions by focusing on the relationship between *feasibility* and *fantasy*. Feasibility has become a very important term in our current lexicon. Before we do anything or launch any program someone must do a "feasibility study." Those responsible for feasibility studies occupy in our time the place once held by the seers and oracles. We consult their data banks, computers, and extrapolation techniques; they no longer rely on the gizzards of birds or the patterns of bones dropped from a bag. Only the foolhardy set out on an enterprise which has not been pronounced feasible by an appropriately trained consultant.

But what does feasible really mean? It means possible of accomplishment in view of the social material and personal resources now at hand or foreseeable. Feasibility thus assumes a future which must grow out of the facts of the present. It discourages our hoping or aspiring toward something which flunks the feasibility test. This limits the sweep of human planning, political action, and cultural innovation.

One unorthodox systems analyst, Hasan Ozbekhan, says it should be the other way around:

> Desirable outcomes, however, should by definition arise from larger sets of ends than the set that is determined by feasibility alone. The range of choice is therefore bigger . . . which . . . is an important consideration. Furthermore the direction of the process—or better, its vector—becomes altered when the choice of ends is given primacy over the logical evolution of the means. A desirable outcome can be imagined and structured in detail as an independent conception of the future—independent, that is, from the powerful restrictions that the present imposes.[2]

How can we reignite the capacity for socio-cultural transcendence, or at least the gift for imagining radically alternative futures, futures which are neither mere extensions of existing conditions nor choices among options which have been found feasible in the light of existing or expected means?

In the past the spinning of visions was one of the functions performed by religion, or at least one type of religion. Of course religion performed and still does perform many other functions. It often simply legitimates existing institutions, personal styles, and patterns of power distribution. This is religion as "the opiate of the masses." But as Marx rightly saw, religion is not only an expression of injustice and suffering, it is also a form of protest against it. Often this protest expresses itself in the vision of a new epoch. The idea of a "messianic era," a new age in the relations of men with each other and with nature, arose quite early in the history of Israel. There are parallels though not equivalents in other religious traditions.

In Christianity this vision of the Kingdom of God or the New Jerusalem has had a rich and stormy career. Sometimes it has acted as a catalyst stimulating the culture to transcend itself and its current values; at other times it has acted as a deterrent to change. What are the conditions under which religion functions in these different ways?

In general there are three ways in which the catalytic power of a social vision of a new world to spark change and innovation is undercut. One way is to *postpone* it entirely to an epoch beyond time and history. One merely waits for it, with patience becoming the primary virtue. Another way is to identify it with a particular desired social institution or set of institutions such that when these are either attained or lost the tension is relaxed. A third way is to declare the religious institution itself the Kingdom of God and to spiritualize or individualize the radical hope until it becomes trivial.

Under the first condition the church becomes a small conventicle patiently enduring the travails of the present and awaiting the coming of the new order. Although it was once believed that early Christianity exemplified this model, recent research on the relation between Jesus and the zealots and the work of Ernst Benz on early

Christianity raises some doubts. The Essene community which produced the Qumram library (the "Dead Sea Scrolls") is a better example. The second pattern has been followed by utopian groups and those who identify Christianity with a particular religio-political ideology for centuries. And the third approach is typical of the Constantinian-Catholic model which was instituted in a modified way in North America.

All three approaches undermine religiously inspired social transcendence. If the new epoch is found only in heaven, in a specially blueprinted state, or in the church, social transcendence—at least that which can be inspired by religion—is lost.

RELIGION AND TRANSCENDENT VISION

How does religion contribute to a society's capacity for social transcendence? It does so by symbolizing an ideal toward which to strive and by doing so with sufficient affective power that the ideal provides a real source of motivation. In order to do this a religion must be able to *change* such that its symbols inspire a society, but remain in *continuity* with the past so that the symbols have credibility. Let us look first at the problem of change in religion.

Since the middle of the nineteenth century theologians in both Catholic and Protestant churches and leading thinkers in Judaism have recognized that religions are not static but do develop historically and do change. It is not surprising that this recognition should have come so late, since the recognition that societies develop and change is also a relatively new realization of Western man. Since societies tend to change more rapidly than the value structures and belief patterns which guide them, it is understandable that religious thinkers should have recognized the changing and developing character of religion rather late. However, even though theologians have recognized religion as a developmental phenomenon, the next crucial step has not been taken: recognizing the need for conscious and planned change in religious systems and patterns of belief.

One of the most significant contributions of Pierre Teilhard de Chardin to recent religious and ethical thinking is his insistence that evolution has now reached a point where man is responsible for the next stage. He registers several stages in cosmic and animal evolution in which certain nodal points such as the emergence of life, of consciousness, and later of self-consciousness are the main ones. His central thesis is that, although the evolutionary process has moved from "within" so far, we have now arrived at a point where "The stuff of the universe has begun to think.[3]" The fact that man must now take charge of the next stage of human and even of cosmic evolution naturally makes Teilhard de Chardin uncomfortable with certain inherited formulations of original sin. In fact, at one point he calls original sin "the iron collar around the neck of man." His ideas, although roundly condemned in recent years by the Vatican, have nonetheless become one of the most important ingredients in contemporary Catholic theology. They also have played an important role in Protestant theology. It is interesting, however, that although he insisted that man must take conscious measures in the next step in the evolution of the species, he nowhere suggests that man must be equally conscious about the next step in the evolution of religion.

The problem is that there is insufficient theological ground for legitimating religious innovation and the conscious development of symbols and belief systems. We do recognize that religions have developed and changed in the past, but generally the conscious innovation in religion has been condemned. The word for such innovation is "heresy." The first major task that theology must undertake in the next decades, therefore, is to work out how conscious innovation and symbol reformulation, even symbol creation, can occur. How are new symbols evaluated? How is their validity to be judged? All of these are questions to which theologians must now address themselves. In all of this it is clear that since experimentation must be encouraged rather than thwarted, the whole concept of heresy has outlived its usefulness.

Innovation also requires a *variety* of experiments going on, a "hundred flowers blooming." Here the picture seems fairly bright. Predictions about the future of religion in the technologized and industrialized world of the twenty-first century vary widely. Some futurologists predict the total disappearance of religion; others say that a single world religion will emerge synthesizing the major elements of existing religions; and others believe that a new religion only marginally similar to existing religious systems but shorn of any mythical or symbolic component will emerge. On the basis of existing trends, however, it seems most likely to me that we will have in the future world a variety of different religious belief systems. It is interesting to point out that in the twenty-three years since the end of the Second World War, the rapid economic and industrial development of Japan has *not* resulted in the disappearance of religion, but has, on the contrary, provided the setting in which an enormous variety of new religious movements has emerged.

Closely related to the problem of the creation of new values is the definition of who man is and what his appropriate task in history should be. Discussions about technology often use such phrases as "dehumanization" and "depersonalization." Obviously these terms cannot be used unless there is an underlying assumption about what it means to be human or to be a person. Close to the heart of the various world religious systems is an understanding of who man is and what his essential relationship to history and the cosmos should be. One of the reasons why it is unlikely that biblical religion can be merged or synthesized with Hindu religion is that these two religious systems project highly divergent notions of man's place in the cosmos and in history. For biblical religion the importance of terrestrial history is far more central than it is for Hinduism. In Christianity God actually "becomes flesh," and therefore earthly realities have a significance which they do not have in the "nonhistorical" religions such as Hinduism. It should be added immediately that this is a simplification of two extremely elaborate symbol systems, and that the recent history of Hinduism suggests a much more serious attitude toward historical realities. Nonetheless there remains a marked contrast between the answers these two religions would give to the question, "What is it that is essential about the human?"

In Christian theology three main answers have been given to that question. Roman Catholic theology, drawing on St. Thomas Aquinas and through him on Aristotle, has tended to emphasize man's reason. Protestant theology, drawing more on St. Augustine, has tended to emphasize man's freedom. The Greek and Russian Orthodox traditions, although their emphasis has been less clear, have leaned more toward the concept of "creativity" as man's distinguishing characteristic.[4]

It would seem that without sacrificing the notions of reason and freedom, Western theology needs to develop far more explicitly the idea of creativity as a distinguishing characteristic of human existence. This means that man does not live in a world which is already finished but rather in an open universe where he has the privilege and responsibility of continuing the process of creation. In fact, the refusal to continue the process of innovation and creation might very well be considered the major form of sin in the contemporary world.

Christianity came into the world as a movement which expected a radically different future and which legitimized a form of behavior which was future-oriented. Certainly the early Christians and the Jews from whom they inherited their messianic posture did not expect the kind of future we expect; nonetheless they were basically a future-oriented people in the midst of a civilization which was by and large oriented toward the past. With the emergence of the Constantinian compromise and the substitution of Christianity for the emperor cultus as the *sacra publica* of the empire, this future-oriented posture of Christianity disappeared. Christianity became the sacral legitimation for the existing institutional structure of the empire, and from the fourth century until relatively recently Christianity has continued to provide the sacral legitimation for the institutions of Western civilization.

From about the sixteenth century until the present another tendency has been at work in Western civilization that has undercut the capacity of Christianity to legitimate cultural values and social institutions. This phenomenon is called secularization. Although it has been feared and criticized by church leaders, secularization really frees biblical religion to assume its original posture of radical expectation and of criticism of the existing institutions in the society. The Roman Catholic theologian Johannes Metz suggests that the church must now become a "meta-critical institution." Certainly secularization means that Christianity will include a smaller minority of persons in the society. It provides, however, the possibility for a reappropriation of the critical, prophetic, and perhaps catalytic function which Christianity once played. Since the institutions of the society no longer need the kind of monolithic sacral legitimation once provided by Christianity, the church is now freed to play a more critical role in the social process.

Here and there throughout the history of Western Christianity movements have appeared which historians have labeled "visionary" or "utopian." Although they have sometimes become heretical, it is possible that these movements now provide a more adequate model for the role of the church in society than the model provided by the Constantinian church. In order to transcend itself society needs a goal which is symbolically powerful but resistant to complete actualization. Only with such a vision will society remain mobile, flexible, and changing. This suggests that the role of religion in society today might become that of the visionary. Drawing on its tradition in the Hebrew scriptures, the early history of Christianity, and the sectarian movements on the edges of the Western church, contemporary Christianity might provide those images and metaphors of a society of the future which would at once stimulate and induce social change without being so specific in their details as to choke off its possibility.

FANTASY AND MADNESS

So far I have discussed the role of religion in helping society achieve self-transcendence mainly in institutional terms. When I turn to look at the individual person, it seems clear that if we wish to regain the kind of radical vision which once inspired men to try to change quality instead of just quantity, we must discard most of what we now believe about "normalcy," "mental illness," and "mental health." If the concept of heresy prevents the church from exercising originality, current notions about mental hygiene operate even more powerfully in a society which is anxiously committed to mental health.

As Dr. Thomas Szasz has made clear in many of his writings, our culture now labors under a constrictive and ideologically narrow conception of what it means to be mentally healthy. Most of our standards of mental hygiene derive from the value assumptions of a late puritan, work-oriented, repressive historical period. We judge psychological deviancy on the basis of a person's relative capacity to operate in this society successfully. We reward people whose personalities lean toward competition, upward mobility, toughness, or even an obsessive need to accumulate material goods. We punish people who experiment with novel living styles, who cultivate esoteric interests or idiosyncratic beliefs. The person whose life ambition is to make a million dollars is lionized; the person who wants to meet God is tolerated; the person who wants to experience a trance is institutionalized.

There can be little doubt that many people need psychiatric care today. It is also true, however, that many people are subjected to incarceration and treatment mainly because their behavior, language, life styles, or beliefs do not comport with the conventional practices of the society. The use of mental health techniques, psychiatric screening, and long periods of "observation" in public institutions to control "deviancy" not only endangers our freedom as citizens; it also snuffs out the sparks of novelty and creativity any society needs in order to remain flexible and innovative.

In his dialogue *Phaedrus,* Plato has Socrates say, "The greatest blessings come by the way of *mania,* insofar as *mania* is heaven-sent" (244-a-6). Ever since there has been a lively discussion in Western thought about what *mania* is, how to tell whether it is "heaven-sent," and how it relates to what we call madness. By and large the notion that "mad" people have something to tell us has been retained by religious people while the medical profession, with some exceptions, has looked upon mania as a sickness to be cured. For Socrates himself the answer was clear. Later on in the *Phaedrus* he speaks of a man possessed by *mania* and says of him, "The multitude regard him as being out of his wits, for they know not that he is full of a god" (249-d-2).

The same problem existed in early Hebrew prophecy. Visionaries and ecstatics might well be simply mad or they might have a word from God, so it was wise to pay attention to them. Until just recently we thought we had solved the problem by deciding that all mania is madness: "deviants" are sick and must be returned to normalcy. I say "until recently" because in the past few years some psychiatrists have begun to suggest not only that the "rantings" of madmen make their own kind of sense, but that society may have much to learn from them. Their experience may not only reveal with poignant vividness the contradictions of the society focused in one person. They may also provide inputs and ideas, styles and aspirations not yet weazened by the heavy hand of feasibility.

Without surrendering to a romanticism of madness we need to develop ways to "test the spirits and see if they be of God." We need to recognize that "normalcy," "health," "feasibility," and even "reality" are historically and socially conditioned constructs. We must listen to the deviants of our society before pronouncing them all kooks. Some of them are. Some may be full of god, that is, full of feeiings, hopes, and insights which still seem insane to our time but just may open fissures toward the future. The Greeks knew this when they relied on the oracles at Delphi and the Sibyl, usually in a state of transport (*theia mania*), to help them think about the future. The Hebrews knew it when they listened to prophets who often had periods of ecstasy. Tribal peoples have had shamans. Other cultures have had saints, poets, and holy men. We tend to see them all as a little odd or to tolerate them on the margins of society. We must now learn to appreciate them more as those without whom we literally have no real future.

CONCLUSION

Our capacity to transcend the limits of some arbitrary definition of "feasibility" in our hopes and aspirations for society may require us to take a closer look at two phenomena we have tended to regard as remnants of a prerational era, visionary religion and "holy" madness. For the health of the whole society some of us may have to become again "fools for Christ."

REFERENCES

1. Fred L. Polak, *The Image of the Future* (Dobbs Ferry, N.Y.: Oceana Publications, 1961).
2. Hasan Ozbekhan, Technology and Man's Future (paper presented at the Symposium on the Technological Society, The Center for the Study of Democratic Institutions, Santa Barbara, California, December 19–23, 1965), p. 14.
3. Pierre Teilhard de Chardin, *The Appearance of Man*, translated by J. M. Cohen (New York: Harper & Row, 1965).
4. See Nicholai Berdyaev, *The Destiny of Man* (London: G. Bles, 1937).

THE LOSS OF THE STABLE STATE
DONALD A. SCHON

I HAVE BELIEVED for as long as I can remember in an afterlife within my own life—a calm, stable state to be reached after a time of troubles. When I was a child, that afterlife was Being Grown Up. As I have grown older, I have found its content more nebulous, but its image, in spite of conscious rejection, has stubbornly persisted.

The afterlife-within-my-life is a form of belief in what I would like to call the Stable State. Belief in the Stable State is belief in the unchangeability, the constancy, of central aspects of our lives, or belief in the attainability of such a constancy. Belief in the Stable State is strong and deep in us. We institutionalize it in every social domain. We do this in spite of our talk about change, our apparent acceptance of change, and our approval of dynamism. Language about change is for the most part talk about very small change, trivial in relation to a massive unquestioned stability, which nevertheless appears formidable to its proponents by the same peculiar optic that leads a potato chip company to see a larger bag of potato chips as a new product. Moreover, talk about change is as often as not a substitute for engaging in it.

Belief in the Stable State is pervasive. We believe in the stability of major elements of our own identities such as our occupations or professions. "I am a chemist," "I am a college professor," "I am a doctor," "I am a short order cook"—we make such judgments not as tentative findings subject to change but as assertions concerning enduring aspects of the self. To be unable to make them or to be ambiguous about them is a matter for some embarrassment.

We believe in the stability of the organizations and institutions with which we are associated ("I work for G.E."), and in the stability of our status or roles within these organizations ("I am director of admissions") and in the stability of the ideology that tends to be associated with them ("At Harvard, we respect individual scholarship," "At the Lighthouse for the Blind, our concern is with human beings, not with numbers"). We believe in the stability of intellectual subject matters or disciplines ("My field is physics," "I have majored in early American history"). We believe in the stability of certain values—for example, those associated with freedom, work, satisfaction, justice, and peace.

Belief in these various Stable States is not always explicit. Often it is implicit or underground. We would not be likely to assert the unchanging character of the General Electric Company, if that were questioned, but members of G.E. act as though its stability was unquestioned. For them the issue of its stability is not likely to arise. We are dealing here with "as if" stability, a stability for all practical purposes.

I would like to make the case that belief in the Stable State is central to our makeup; it is central because it is a bulwark against the threat of uncertainty. Given the reality of change, we can maintain belief in the Stable State only through tactics of which we are largely unaware. Within recent years our responses to attacks on the Stable State are responses of desperation, largely destructive and largely unconscious. Our need, therefore, is to develop an ethic for the process of change itself.

THE FUNCTION OF BELIEF IN THE STABLE STATE

Belief in the Stable State is pervasive. We believe in the stability hension of the threats inherent in change.

The components of organizational, institutional, and intellectual life are arrayed in systems such that changes in one component tend to entrain changes elsewhere in the system. Changes can be pictured in a kind of target diagram in which those closest to the periphery are least critical and those closest to the center are most critical to the organization of beliefs, attitudes, and values that constitutes the "self." A change in beliefs about foreign relations may, for one person, be trivial in its impact on the self; but change in beliefs about the place that is his home may have significant impact. And change in belief and attitude toward his status in his family, or toward the way he is seen by others, may be broadly disruptive.

W. V. Quine has proposed a way of accounting for the greater and lesser centrality of propositions—for propositions that are axioms of logic, for example, as against propositions about matters of fact—and as an alternative to the binary distinction between synthetic and analytic propositions.

> . . . the more fundamental a law is to our conceptual scheme, the less likely we are to choose it for revision. When some revision of our system of statements is called for, we prefer, other things being equal, a revision which disturbs the system least. . . . The priority on law, considered now apart from any competition with the priority on statements verified by experience, admits of many gradations. Conjectures of history and economics will be revised more willingly than laws of physics, and these more willingly than laws of mathematics and logic. . . . Mathematics and logic, central as they are to the conceptual scheme, tend to be accorded such immunity, in view of our conservative preference for revisions which disturb the system least; and herein, perhaps, like the "necessity" which the laws of mathematics and logic are felt to enjoy.[2]

Elting Morison has pointed out the systems character of relationships between technology and the social systems built around technology as a way of accounting for forms of resistance to technological change.

> Military organizations are societies built around and upon the prevailing weapons systems. Intuitively and quite correctly the military man feels that a change in weapons portends a change in the arrangements of his society . . . if the ship is displaced as the principal element by such a radically different weapon as the plane. . . . The mores and structure of the society are immediately placed in jeopardy. . . .[3]

A change that may not appear threatening in itself, therefore—such as a change in the technology of continuous aim firing or a change in belief about rules of evidence—may emerge as threatening because of the additional changes it would entrain. The threat in a change is related to its centrality in the systems of knowledge, or of organizations and institutions which would be affected by it. But threats to organizations and institutions affect individuals because of this age in which individual beliefs, values, and senses of identity are tied up in social systems. In the last analysis, the degree of threat presented by a change depends on its connection to the self, to self-identity.

Life crises, as Erik Erikson and others have explained, center around periods of change or transition in which urgent questions of identity are raised. The transition from infancy to the period in which the child learns to say "I," the beginning of school, puberty, entry into work, marriage, menopause and climacteric, retirement—these are all periods of tension and testing, more or less traumatic. Entry into and release from the army, widowhood, the "decompression" attendant on return from public life—these are less universal transitions characterized by uneasiness or disruption.

Unexpected instability may be more traumatic than predictable changes. The marriage that refuses to "settle down," a change of career, the experience of a woman abandoned by her children, a young college graduate still unsure of what he wants to do, a mature man still plagued by the questions of his adolescence: in these situations the pain of the instability is magnified by the feeling that "I am not supposed to be experiencing this now."

The threat inherent in change is even clearer when we turn from the span of an individual's or an organization's life to our perception of objects in space and time. Philosophers and psychologists, at least as far back as David Hume, have shown how our apprehension of objects and of causality are constructs won, out of the flux of experience, through the active management of experience. Regularities of experience, however we understand them, are central to our apprehension of real objects and ultimately to our sanity. A stream of experience in which expectations are continually disappointed permits no grasp on reality and leads to a kind of insanity, as experiments with sensory deprivation and with the presentation of ambiguous stimuli suggest. Our grasp on reality depends on the stable regularity of perception. In some instances, at least, insanity may be understood as a last-ditch effort to gain this regularity in situations which militate against it.

All experiences threatening change have in common the situa-

tion of uncertainty. I do not mean "risk," which is in effect a probability ratio describing the likely occurrence of some future event,
but the situation of being at sea, of being lost, of confronting more
information than one can handle.

Uncertainty arises in a variety of settings. I come to be truly confused about interpreting the behavior of someone who, until now,
has been close to me. His act appears hostile, but may be quite different. How am I to understand this? How shall I respond to him?
A psychotherapist who has been working with a patient suddenly
finds himself confronted with behavior that belies his way of seeing
the patient with which he has been working—and there is, as yet, no
alternative hypothesis in sight. A business firm begins to perceive
that its product line and its marketing policy are inadequate to the
demands of the market. The market does not respond to the firm's
tested strategies of recovery. A scientist, committed to a cherished
hypothesis, encounters data which do not fit—and which present
no clear alternative pattern. A scientific community—such as the
community of physicists in the early years of this century, or the
community of nuclear physicists in the last decade—find an entire
conceptual framework inadequate to the data presented by a program of experiments which cannot be discredited or abandoned.

In these situations there is not a lack of information; there is no
"information gap." There is an information overload, too many sig-
nals, more than can be accounted for; and there is as yet no theory
in terms of which new information can be sought or new experiments undertaken. Uncertainty is a way of talking about the situation in which no plausible theory has emerged.

For this reason pragmatism is no response.[4] We cannot, in these
situations, say "Let us get the data," "Let us experiment," "Let us
test," for there is as yet nothing to test. Out of the uncertainty, out of
the experience of a bewildering array of information, new hypotheses
must emerge, and from them mandates for data gathering, testing,
and experiment, can be derived. But the hypotheses do not in the
first instance exist. Their existence is a condition for the application
of the method of pragmatism. The period of uncertainty must be
traversed *in order that* pragmatism may become an appropriate
response.

The feeling of uncertainty is anguish. The depth of anguish

increases as the threatening changes strike at more central regions of the self. It is most severe in what Ronald Laing has called onto-logical uncertainty.

> The individual in the ordinary circumstances of living may feel more unreal than real; in a literal sense, more dead than alive; precariously differentiated from the rest of the world, so that his identity and autonomy are always in question. He may lack the experience of his own temporal continuity. He may not possess an over-riding sense of personal consistency or cohesiveness. He may feel more insubstantial than substantial, and unable to assume that the stuff he is made of is genuine, good, valuable. And he may feel his self as partially divorced from his body.[5]

Against all of this, we have erected our belief in the Stable State.

TACTICS FOR MAINTENANCE OF BELIEF IN THE STABLE STATE

The norm in experience is flux and variety. Surprises are constantly occurring. The unexpected is the rule. If we limit ourselves to American experience, for the moment, we can make a good case that we have always been in process and affirmative toward change, that we have never had a national Stable State. What is curious is not that we are forced at intervals to abandon some Stable State, but that we managed to acquire belief in it in the first place.

The process by which we maintain this belief is not a passive or inertial resistance but an active and more or less systematic response. Our defense against uncertainty is a dynamic conservatism in which we engage, concurrently, in a number of strategies.

We are selectively inattentive to the data that would upset our current way of looking at things. We need look no further for an illustration than the prodigious effort by which most middle class white Americans have succeeded for decades in failing to perceive the quality of Negro American experience that has been under our noses all the time. It is indeed characteristic of every discovery, in whatever domain, that we are astonished at not having "seen it" earlier.

We manage a kind of internal economy in which changes in one domain find compensation in stability in others. The "private lives" of inventors, innovators, artists, and discoverers are typically regular to the point of dull routine, and that dullness is apt to be jealously guarded. We undertake an active program of maintenance of the homeostatic system in which we are involved, whether it is the system of the firm, the family, or the self. This often takes the form of hostile resistance, overt or underground, to whatever threatens to break up the stable system. Where we cannot help but perceive the change we strive actively to contain or suppress it. Instances are to be found in the patient's resistance to psychotherapy, the neighborhood's expulsion of troublesome outsiders, the business firm's elaboration of systems for the control of innovations, and the governmental bureaucracies' magnificent semi-conscious system for the long-term wearing down of agents of change. The effort spent in all of these maneuvers may be as unconscious as the effort of keeping balance in a sailboat.

THE NATURE OF THE THREAT TO BELIEF IN THE STABLE STATE

What is apparent now is the extent to which the attack on the Stable State is beyond the capability of our strategies of resistance or containment. Throughout our society we are experiencing the actual or threatened dissolution of stable organizations and institutions, anchors for personal identity, and systems of values which have been central for us. Most important, the concept of the Stable State itself has become less real for us.

There is no established organization which does not now feel itself inadequate to the challenges that face it. The nature of the American business firm is in serious question, in spite of the unquestionable prosperity and vitality of American business. Traditional concepts of "my business" (the shoe business or the office equipment business, for example) have come to seem inadequate through the same process by which traditional pyramidal, bounded concepts of the form of business organizations have dissolved. The change has been multidetermined. It has come from pressures for growth and the saturation of markets following World War II, from the evolution of the concept of research and of what it means to be a research-based firm, and from the industrial invasions to which businesses have had to respond by shifting both their form and their concept of the business they are in. Network and constellation structures are replacing the pyramid. Open-ended or process-oriented concepts of "our business" are replacing substantive notions like "shoes" or "office equipment."

The American Labor Movement suffers from what the more articulate of its leaders are calling a failure of success. Its achievement of the goals of the thirties, which gave Labor its vitality, have left it with a sickening feeling of becoming, not a vital force for social change in America, but another bureaucratic institution. Labor leaders complain, "We are becoming middle class." The young men coming up in the organization look to the older leaders like young men rising in any bureaucracy; they could be members of middle management in business or the civil service.

The Federal Government, divided in its executive branch into established agencies, comes to resemble assemblage of memorials to old problems: the Department of Labor, to the problems of unemployment of the thirties; the Department of Agriculture, to the problems of agricultural productivity of the late nineteenth and early twentieth centuries. New problems come to be perceived, but the structures of old agencies and the social systems built around them stand in the way of effective response. Interagency committees, reorganizations and mergers, and the creation of new agencies on the model of the old all fail in various ways to solve adequately the problem of how we are to manage Federal response to new problems that cut across old organizational boundaries without creating new memorials which will come, in turn, to present the same problems all over again.

Universities have found themselves caught among conflicting pressures. They are urged by the Government to assume new roles, nationally and regionally, for which they are ill prepared and with which their traditional ideals of scholarship and liberal education conflict. Students press them for new distributions of power, new concepts of education more relevant to the demands of the world outside the university. Goals relating to meeting the increasing demand for higher education, preparation for a vocation, and financial autonomy all compete, while the goals of education and the role of the university in our society seem hopelessly confused.

The church, in its various guises, asks itself questions which sound more and more like the self-investigation of business firms. How can we become more relevant to our client groups? How do we determine what is expected of us—and the role we can usefully play—in the alignment of new institutions? How do we cast off old structures and forms of organization without coming apart at the seams? How do we introduce measured change without precipitating revolution?

Open revolt, disaffection, indifference, and the appearance of undergrounds and guerilla groups challenge an establishment which feels increasingly threatened over the viability of its traditional heritage of intellectual content and of spiritual mission. Are these troubling events to be seen as signs of decay or as intimations of new vitality? This inventory of threatened institutions, each in the grip of an instability it understands only imperfectly, could be elaborated in depth and breadth. Enough has been said, perhaps, to indicate that we are experiencing a general rather than an isolated or peripheral phenomenon.

The threat to the stability of established institutions is notable, in addition, because of the linkage of institutional stability to the stability of associated intellectual and ideological systems. The business firm, like the Labor Movement, the university, the church, and the service institution, carries with it a body of theory which constitutes a way of looking at the world and an ideology that shapes stance and action. The perceived instability of the institution threatens its accompanying theory and ideology, loosening the anchors for identity which it provided. The net effect is a contribution to the assault on the stability of the self.

The widespread sense of inadequacy to present challenges on the part of institutions throughout our society and the widespread erosion of anchors for personal identity come from phenomena that are in some sense special or unique to our time. But it is not easy to characterize these phenomena with precision. Statements about the increased rate of technological or social change fall flat. It can be argued that rates of change in our society are no more precipitous than they have been at any time during the last two hundred years. Moreover, there are examples of societies, like the Japanese, that have in the last hundred years experienced unparalleled rates of technological and economic change and have somehow managed in that process to preserve the essential structure of their institutions and values, at least until very recently.

A more promising line of thought would appear to be this: Technological and technology-related changes, proceeding at rates normal for the last two hundred years, have in the last thirty to fifty years reached critical levels. They have exceeded critical thresholds for institutions and for individuals.

To take one particularly important example, the frequency of technological impacts on society and of responsive changes in social systems has reached the point where adaptation cannot remain generational. Problems of adaptation that could have been handled—say in the period between 1800 and 1920—through the conflict of generations and the replacement of one generation by another must now be handled within a single generation. We are no longer able to afford the process composed of equal parts of selective inattention to change and of gradual, unconscious adaptation, resulting in the maintenance of the illusion of the Stable State.

Again, as McLuhan has pointed out most effectively, the character of the electronic technology peculiar to our time has been unique in its effect on our institutions and values. Quite apart from questions of increase in rate of change, we have been confronted with a technology of communication and interaction that has been implosive in its effects on our society, moving toward the limit of instantaneous confrontation of every part of our society with every other part.

Both of these features of sociotechnical process peculiar to our time have encouraged the creation of a special sort of skepticism. When we are forced to confront institutions, structures, and values radically different from our own, when we are forced repeatedly to make radical transitions in our own lives, we are led to doubt the special status or stability of our own present institutional, structural, and normative solutions.

Emil Fackenheim has described one aspect of this skepticism.

In this historically self-conscious age, few men can ever forget that what seems unquestionably true to one age or civilization differs from what seems unquestionably true to others. And from historical self-consciousness there is but one step—albeit a long and fateful one—to a wholesale historical scepticism: to the despairing view that history discloses a variety of conflicting *Weltanschauungen,* with no criterion for choice between them anywhere in sight.[6]

RESPONSES TO THE LOSS OF THE STABLE STATE

Two questions arise in a context in which the Stable State institutions, values, and anchors for identity in our society no longer seem adequate, and we appear to have lost faith in the Stable State itself: How can we maintain our sense of self-respect while in the process of change? How can our institutions manage to confront their challenges without flying apart at the seams? Responses in good currency seem to vary along the following dimensions.

Return—the response of reaction against the anguishing present. Recently I heard an old farmer in Oklahoma say that he had been farming for forty years and felt he had become something of an expert on the subject. It was his considered opinion that the farmer had gone from milking 10 to 20 to 40 cows without increasing his income. He was only running to stand still. All this was the fault of the Agricultural Extension Service and of technological progress in general. Sooner or later we would have to return to the concept of the family farm.

Localism is a special case of the response of "return." It is an attempt to enforce and sustain isolation from the phenomena that threaten established institutions and values. Since the desired past survives in an enclave, the drive to return takes the form of an attempt to protect the integrity of that enclave—as in the State of Mississippi at the present time.

Revolt. The revolutionary response is toward total rejection of the past, against the past incarnated in existing social systems. Castro, Fanon, and Che are the revolutionary culture heroes of black revolutionaries in the United States and of students in revolt throughout the world. The characteristic movement of revolution is against established institutions rather than toward a vivid and well-worked-out ideal. In this sense, direction comes from the established institutions themselves and the past sneaks in the back door.

Eric Hoffer points out,

> In reality the boundary line between radical and reactionary is not always distinct. The reactionary manifests radicalism when he comes to recreate his ideal past. His image of the past is based less on what it actually was than on what he wants the future to be. He innovates more than he reconstructs. A somewhat similar shift occurs in the case of the radical when he goes about building his new world. He feels the need for practical guidance, and since he has rejected and destroyed the present he is compelled to link the new world with some point in the past. . . .[7]

Revolt moves against, sustaining energy as long as there is a target. Throughout American society there is a movement for those without power, of all kinds and in all domains of society—the old, children, the disabled, the mentally ill, as well as the blacks and students—to revolt against oppressive established institutions. There is attraction to the process of revolution.

Mindlessness is an attempt to escape from anguish and uncertainty by evading reflective consciousness itself. The means may be drugs, hypnotic routine, violence, or a peculiar union with machine technology, like the kids in midwestern American towns who tool around empty squares at night on motorcycles or in hot rods and seem to be saying, "The machine is winning. Why not join it?"

Fackenheim, after describing the historical skepticism I have quoted above, outlines three responses to it which make an interesting counterpoint to what I have so far suggested.

> The first [of three contemporary attitudes] is what may be called *skeptical paralysis*. Here historical self-consciousness has led to two results: to the insight that wherever there has been a great purpose there has been a great faith; and to the loss of capacity for commitment to such a faith. Hence there is paralysis which recognizes itself as paralysis and preaches doom.

Then there is what may be called *pragmatic make-believe.*
Here . . . [man] falls to pretending to believe hoping that a
pretended might do the work of an actual faith. But it cannot. . . .
When men truly suffer from this contradiction they may seek escape in the most ominous form of modern spiritual life: *ideological fanaticism* . . . ideology asserts itself absolutely . . . it knows
itself to be not truth but merely one specific product of history.
. . . Hence unlike faith, ideology must by its very nature become
fanatical . . . ideology can achieve certainty only by *making* itself
true.[8]

What I have called the responses of Return and Revolt take the
form of ideological fanaticism. My description of them comes, I
think, from my having fastened on our sense of loss of stability
rather than historical skepticism as the dominant feature of our present condition. Skeptical paralysis and pragmatic make-believe join
with mindlessness as responses (inherently unstable responses, I
think) to the loss of the Stable State.

Paul Goodman, who is concerned in *Growing Up Absurd* with
many of these same themes, has a different response:

Modern times have been characterized by fundamental changes
occurring with unusual rapidity. These have shattered tradition but
often have not succeeded in creating a new whole community. We
have no recourse to going back, there is nothing to go back to. *If we
are to have a stable and whole community, we must painfully perfect
the revolutionary modern tradition we have.*[9]

Goodman's revolt is different in that he has a remarkably clear view
of the state toward which revolt should move. And his vision is in
many ways an eighteenth century vision of freedom, order, peace,
individuality, and creativity. It is Revolt with a program, and
Return without reaction. But, without slurring his marvelous critique of contemporary society, it is difficult to believe in the stability of the ideal condition he depicts. And Goodman himself seems
to be saying that the young require belief in a Stable State ("the
ideal toward which I am growing") but that adults must learn to
"confront an uninvented and undiscovered present."

This suggests another kind of response, which differs from any of
those sketched above. What is called for is an ethic of change tran-

scending substantive ethics, providing an alternative to Return or Revolt, and to the various escapist responses by developing felt norms for the process of change itself. It would be an ethic for the process by which we move from one Stable State (of beliefs, attitudes, worldviews, values) to others through zones of uncertainty, while yet retaining a sense of identity and stability which would not require adherence to ways of seeing or feeling that had become hollow and inadequate.

AN ETHIC FOR CHANGE

An ethic for change rests on a Hericlitan imperative: Change, in response to changing situations! The ground of the imperative is in our experience of the consequences of an affected stability in the midst of changing situations; it is in everything that has been said up to this point. Its implications constitute an unfolding of an ethic for change.

Commitment to change implies the priority of the here-and-now. Commitment to the literal past is the enemy of change. Our "rear view mirror," in McLuhan's phrase, works against change. Speculation about the future without engagement in the here-and-now also circumvents change. It is language about what might be, without involvement in the present through action creative of what will be.

Engagement in the here-and-now is not "living for the present." It is not aesthetic enjoyment of the now or "present pleasure," although it may produce a kind of joy. The dynamic conservatism of the self and of the institutions in which the self exists runs counter to enjoyment in the here-and-now; discipline is required to overcome that current.

The priority of the here-and-now requires commitment to the continual testing of ways of looking at and valuing the world. A "transcendent value" undiscoverable in the here-and-now is not a value for me. It is the illusion of a value, the hope or "cover" of a value.

If I am a "professional," then my professionalism should be discoverable now, in this situation; it should not be an after-the-fact professionalism projected onto some future state. If honesty and openness are my values, they should be discoverable now, in this situation. If they are not available to me in this way, they are not part of me. If I am contributive, then my contribution is to be found now, not in a reading of past contribution as a gloss onto present performance.

Commitment to the here-and-now requires commitment to radical experiment. It requires openness to discovery and to loss. We can no longer count on the safety afforded by resolving to maintain our convictions even to the point of ignoring or suppressing the givens of a present situation.

By the same token, commitment to the priority of the here-and-now implies a kind of faith in the self as discoverable. Willingness to put ways of looking at the world to the test in the here-and-now signifies faith in the solidity of the self. This is not faith in the self as preformed and available before a given situation; it is faith in the undiscovered self.

Openness to the present situation may force a coming apart of the self. Commitment to the here-and-now implies a faith in one's ability to break apart and to come together again in new ways. Moreover, this is a faith in one's own undiscovered resources. The story of Humpty Dumpty can be seen as an allegory of the fragile egg-self made brittle by its fear of the here-and-now. He falls, rather than leaps, into the present; others cannot put him together again.

Fear of failure, anguish, and uncertainty; fear of loss of self or an aspect of the self, such as the concept of the self as successful, prestigeful or familiar; fear of the dissolution or breaking of the self—these stand as obstacles to engagement in the here-and-now. There is a kind of freedom attached to the willingness to risk the self. It is the feeling of adequacy to any challenge, not in the sense of confidence in victory over it but in strength to meet it.

The here-and-now is essentially an interpersonal here-and-now. When one submits an aspect of the self to the test of the here-and-now, it is always at least in part to the test of the reaction of others. This is far more than the fortuitous presence of others in some present situation. It is a feature of the dependence of the concept of the self on the notion of significant others as that concept has been formulated, for example, by George Herbert Mead and Harry Stack Sullivan. Sullivan defines the "self-system" as "the system involved in the maintenance of felt interpersonal security."[10] And

Mead defines the self in terms of "internalized others." In that sense, the here-and-now for me, even when I am alone, is an interpersonal one.

The test of a belief, a value, an aspect of the self-image, is not in the here-and-now agreement of others. It is in the ability of that aspect of the self to be sustained and made real in the presence of others. In our society it is unusual and anxiety-producing to display uncertainty before others, to come apart in public, to speak before we have anything to say. Commitment to the interpersonal here-and-now at times requires these things.

At the close of a chapter on the introduction of continuous aim firing into the American Navy, Elting Morison makes the following comment:

> . . . we might give some attention to the construction of a new view of ourselves as a society which in time of great change identified with and obtained security and satisfaction from the wise and creative accommodation to change itself. Such a view rests, I think, upon a relatively greater reverence for the mere *process* of living in a society, than we possess today, and a relatively smaller respect for and attachment to any special *product* of a society, a product either as finite as a bathroom fixture or as conceptual as a fixed and final definition of our Constitution or our democracy.
>
> . . . We seem to have fallen on times . . . when many of the existing forms and schemes have lost meaning in the face of dramatically altering circumstances . . . . we may find at least part of our salvation in identifying ourselves with the adaptive process. . . .[11]

In this usage Morison already extends the term "product" well beyond its conventional technological or consumer application to encompass conceptual products. I would like to extend the term further still to any fixed or stable entity resulting from action, that is, to anything regarded after the fact as done. In this sense an ethic for change is an ethic for process rather than for product. Moreover, it is an ethic which places a priority on process. It sees process as the enduring background against which transient foreground products come and go. It sees the principal problem of design as the design of process to meet many criteria, among them the accomplishment of certain ends. An ethic for change develops criteria for process and places imperatives on it, as a substantive ethic places imperatives on acts, intentions, or "wills." Commitment to the here-and-now is an important feature of such a process-oriented ethic for change.

This does not, however, imply the need to enter into an unstructured world of pure process, bereft of substantive values, firm perceptions, and solid objects. On the contrary, it implies acceptance of whatever solid beliefs, perceptions, and values are available. But it implies their acceptance as *proximate* values. They are to be taken with whatever assurance can be mustered out of the present situations in which they are tested. But they are expected to change. And when they do, attention must shift to the process in which new values emerge and are tested.

It can be, in 1970, a vital goal for the American Labor Movement to bring workers to the point where many of them are highly technically trained and have a say in management. But the goal is clearly one of limited stability. The nature of work, affected in particular by the character of changing technology, seems likely to change out from under the goals of Labor. If the massive dislocation of workers as a result of technological change is not a significant problem in 1970, it is likely to be one by 1975.

The fading or disruption of goals within their presumed period of stability plunges us into zones of uncertainty, much as the explosion of a hypothesis plunges a scientist or therapist into uncertainty. It is at this point that the priority of the here-and-now, as one aspect of a commitment to values for process, comes into high relief. An ethic for change regards these zones of uncertainty as expectable and presents norms for their confrontation. It rejects their suppression, for example, by making them taboo, or it attempts to evade them by selective inattention or by the devices of Return and Revolt. It demands engagement in them, endurance of the anguish attendant on them, and faith in the potential for discovery inherent in them.

The way of looking at goals, beliefs, and values implicit in what has been said above is not a familiar one in our society. It is normal to regard goals, beliefs, and values as fixed—at least for their implicit periods of stability—and to be surprised and disrupted by their shifts. Such an attitude is inherent in the viewpoint and ethic of the Stable State. But an ethic for change requires attention to process and treats values for process as more enduring than values within process.

There is a kind of paradox in all of this. In order to give priority to process and to the here-and-now, we must regard beliefs, values, and goals as ways of seeing only. "Ways of seeing" implies openness to the notion that others may see differently and with validity; it implies openness to change of vision with change in situation or point of view. But meaningful thought and action demand some engagement in what is believed, felt, or valued. We are asked to be open, not tentative. Otherwise, the recognition that everything is a way of seeing serves as a hedge against any commitment and ultimately against any valid action. This is a form of the skeptical paralysis to which Fackenheim refers. It is akin to the multiple visions of the same situation presented in *Rashomon* or to Hamlet's paralyzing vision of multiple possibilities. What is required is engagement in a point of view while retaining the insight that it is a point of view.

A number of roles in our society incorporate an emphasis on change and process, and with that emphasis, an implicit or explicit ethic of change.

Artist, inventor, scientific discoverer, and therapist all represent engagement with processes of change and depend on the priority of the here-and-now. This priority in each instance has to do with the priority given to discovery—to finding new things, developing new ways of seeing. It is customary to see these roles and their products as radically different from one another, even to the point of identifying some of them (the sciences and arts and humanities, for example) as belonging to different cultures. But to the extent that process and norms for process come to light, these separate experiences seem to be more similar than disparate. They are different in subject matter and environment but radically similar in process.

The compartmentalization of these roles cuts us off systematically from insights into their similarity. The work of an artist, scientist, inventor, or therapist tends to be shut off from the rest of society and not infrequently insulated from the rest of the life experience of the artist, inventor, scientist, or therapist himself.

The artist tends to be isolated in his garret, the inventor in his shop or cellar, the scientist in his laboratory, the therapist in his consulting room. We know these men not by their process but by their products. And, characteristically, we make the mistake of identifying art, invention, science, or therapy as works of art, inventions, scientific papers, or therapeutic results, rather than as the processes of artistry, inventing, discovery, or therapy. There is a resulting tendency to ignore or to mystify the process of the maker; in any case, to be unable to learn from it.

But on the assumption that there is no Stable State and that ordinary human life must aspire to an ethic of change, a search for the conditions of the emergence of novelty and engagement in the process of discovery must come to be the norm rather than the exception for human beings. What used to be peculiar to the process of artist, inventor, or scientist—and then only to the working of his *professional* role—must extend broadly to human life. Life must take on the explicit character of the creative process. From this point of view, it is disastrous for the creative makers in our society to be compartmentalized, for they are the principal sources of learning for an ethic of change.

The role of the jazz musician must then stand out. He improvises, and in so doing plays out in public what is usually kept hidden and revealed only in its results. The growing public interest in improvisational and participative forms of music, theatre, small group experiments, and in the visual and plastic arts represents perhaps a growing awareness of our need for learning about the emergence of novelty.

In *Growing Up Absurd,* Paul Goodman lays down three conditions for the emergence of novelty: energy, security to confront anxiety and uncertainty, and rejection of the past. But surely there is something wrong about the flat phrase "rejection of the past," especially given Goodman's recognition of the essentially conservative thrust of much innovation.

> . . . If we are to have a stable and whole community in which the young can grow to manhood, we must painfully perfect the revolutionary modern tradition we have.

> This stoical resolve is, paradoxically, a *conservative* proposition, aiming at stability and social balance. For often it is not a ques-

tion of making innovations, but of catching up and restoring the right proportions. But no doubt, in our runaway, one-sided way of life, the proposal to conserve human resources and develop human capabilities has become a radical innovation.[12]

I have tried to show elsewhere that the emergence of novelty requires a special use of the past—neither a literal clinging to familiar concepts nor an admission of them through the back door via Revolt, but a use of them as metaphor or projective model for present situation.[13] An ethic for change requires commitment to the conditions for the emergence of novelty and requires, therefore, commitment not to a rejection of the past per se but to a rejection of it as a literal guide to the present situation and an acceptance of it as a projective model for the here-and-now.

Walter Reuther's recent concept of the community union is a case in point. It is an idea responsive to Reuther's sense of Labor's loss of steam and purpose. It reflects a conviction that Labor must remain a leader of social action in America as well as a sense that the site for action has expanded to include community as well as factory or farm. "Community union" is a metaphor whose precise meaning is in the process of working itself out through experiments such as those under way in the California grape country. The metaphor is a way of trying to make relevant to current social action the historical union experience of organization, strike, protest, battle, and bargaining. In the California experiment, all of these terms will come to have a different meaning. But the concept of community union is a way of providing a solid framework out of union history as a starting point for transformation in present situations of social action.

As institutions and individuals ask what they might be if they were not what they are, they are incapable of starting from scratch. They must find some way to build on where they have been, to make aspects of their pasts relevant to present situations. These efforts are reflected in metaphors like Community Union, or New Frontier, which represent not a rejection of the past but its use as a projective model for the present.

An ethic for change is an alternative, the only presently viable alternative, to the views and values of the deteriorating Stable State. The remarks made above suggest that its content will emerge in the effort to resolve certain apparent antinomies: the demand for security in situations of uncertainty and anguish which threaten the security of the self; the demand for conviction and engagement, and with it the requirement that beliefs and values be recognized as ways of looking at the world; engagement with others, with ultimate reliance on the self recognized as the internalization of others; the priority of process over product, but with acceptance of such products as survive the test of the here-and-now; and the rejection of the literal past and acceptance of the past as a projective model for present situations.

The elaboration of an ethic for change appropriate to the demands of our society is not an individual's philosophical enterprise, though making an aspect of it explicit may well be so. It is, if I am right, an enterprise in which our society is now implicitly engaged. It is in the air.

REFERENCES

1. This essay is an attempt to develop ideas originally worked out with the late Dr. Raymond M. Hainer.
2. *Methods of Logic* (New York: Henry Holt & Co., 1960), p. xiii.
3. *Men, Machines and Modern Times* (Cambridge, Mass.: MIT Press, 1966), p. 36.
4. I use the word "pragmatism" here to mean that theory of knowledge or inquiry that assumes the possibility of the generation of convergent empirically based knowledge of the world, gained through a process that includes the gathering of data, the generation of hypotheses to explain these data, the formulation and running of experiments to test hypotheses, and the reformulation of hypotheses on the basis of experimental evidence. The assumption underlying pragmatism, in this sense, is that iterations of the process converge toward knowledge of reality. A "particular pragmatism" is a particular complex of data, hypotheses, and experiments. This use is derived from Dr. Raymond M. Hainer's *Rationalism and Pragmatism* and *Existentialism*, as is much else in this essay.
5. *The Divided Self* (Pelican Books, 1965), p. 42.
6. *Metaphysics and Historicity* (Milwaukee: Marquette University Press, 1961), p. 3.
7. *The True Believer* (New York: Mentor Books, 1951), p. 71.
8. *Metaphysics and Historicity, op. cit.*, pp. 4–7.
9. *Growing Up Absurd* (New York: Vintage Books, 1956), p. 231.
10. *The Interpersonal Theory of Psychiatry* (New York: W. W. Norton, 1953), pp. 108–109.
11. *Men, Machines and Modern Times, op. cit.*, pp. 43–44.
12. *Growing Up Absurd, op. cit.*, pp. 231–232.
13. *Displacement of Concepts* (New York: Tavistock Press, 1963).

TRANSCENDENCE IN CONTEMPORARY PIETY

ROBERT N. BELLAH

We believe without belief, beyond belief [1]—Wallace Stevens.

IN TRADITIONAL THEOLOGY Transcendence is an attribute of God that indicates he is outside and independent of the world. A number of metaphysical arguments have been developed over the centuries to prove this point. Biblical and Quranic religions have also asserted, on the basis of revelation, the existence of God outside the world.

Arguments based on metaphysical proofs or revelation are not very compelling today. These approaches may be viewed as interesting "perspectives" that can be illuminating if properly interpreted in some contemporary frame of reference. It is not so much the substance of what is claimed to be transcendent as it is the *function of the claim itself* that is of interest now. There is a parallel here, for example, with the present state of the discussion of original sin. The idea of original sin may be accepted as an essential perspective on human nature without believing at all St. Augustine's involved bio-theological argument about it.

What, then, is the central function of the idea of Transcendence that may make it worth retaining even though traditional arguments for it must be abandoned? If, in terms of twentieth century cosmology, it is no longer meaningful to retain the idea of anything being, at least in a physico-spatial sense, "outside the world," it still seems essential to appreciate that there is a reality independent of ourselves, our societies, and our cultures:

> From this the poem springs: that we live in a place
> That is not our own and, much more, not ourselves
> And hard it is in spite of blazoned days. [2]

"Reality" has in fact become a highly charged word with a definite overtone of Transcendence, especially in the writings of Freud, whose famous contrast between the reality and pleasure principles emphasizes the "overagainstness" of reality. It is to Wallace Stevens, however, that I wish to turn repeatedly in this essay. As the greatest American "theological poet" of this century he may be particularly useful in helping us to discern the structure of contemporary religious consciousness. In the following passages we can see Stevens giving his own interpretation to certain theological perspectives:

> The theologians whose thought is most astir today do make articulate a supreme need, and one that has now become also imperative, as their urgency shows, the need to infuse into the ages of enlightenment an awareness of reality adequate to their achievements and such as will not be attenuated by them. There is one most welcome and authentic note; it is the insistence on a reality that forces itself upon our consciousness and refuses to be managed and mastered. It is here that the affinity of art and religion is most evident today. Both have to mediate for us a reality not ourselves. This is what the poet does. The supreme virtue here is humility, for the humble are they that move about the world with the love of the real in their hearts.[3] And the wonder and mystery of art, as indeed of religion in the last resort, is the revelation of something "wholly other" by which the inexpressible loneliness of thinking is broken and enriched.[4]

It is worth noting the element of piety in Stevens' words. (I am using "piety" not in its pejorative sense but to indicate an element of action which "religion" does not convey and for which "religious behavior" or "religious action" or even Wilfred Smith's helpful suggestion, "religiousness," seems a bit too clumsy.) For "reality" as an ultimate term has its own religious pathology. With respect to it, too, can occur what Tillich called "the sin of religion," namely, the identification of God's will with one's own. This is usually what the "realist" does when he seeks to justify himself: "I was only being realistic." But such a "realist" lacks humility; he does not love the real in his heart. He lacks a Stevensian piety.

If the notion of reality is the first thing to be said in connection with the contemporary sense of Transcendence, it is certainly not the last. That concept alone is too crude and undifferentiated. Stevens himself offers some further considerations about it to which we shall return later. We first need to develop a series of levels in terms of which the idea of reality may yield various meanings.

THE SELF

Reality may be encountered in the self as well as in the "external" world. St. Augustine said, "Men go to gape at mountain peaks, at the boundless tides of the sea, the broad sweep of rivers, the encircling ocean and the motions of the stars: and yet they leave themselves unnoticed; they do not marvel at themselves."[5] He argued that we should begin our search for God "within." But in those vast inner regions that we can never know completely Augustine recognized other realities besides the divine: "For no one is known to another so intimately as he is known to himself, and yet no one is so well known even to himself that he can be sure as to his conduct on the morrow."[6] The heights and depths of the inner life have been among the central realities of religious men in many times and cultures. The overwhelming reality of the inner life precludes any simple use of the word "subjective," as though the inner life were less "real" than external things. Above all, the inner life is not a matter of personal whim or simple control of the ego. Its "constraining" nature, its "objectivity," makes it a vehicle for Transcendence.

It is precisely with respect to unsatisfied desires and longings which overwhelm all men at certain times and largely dominate the existence of many that the "externality" of the inner life is most pronounced. These "deficiency needs," to use Maslow's term,[7] have by and large been viewed negatively by the great religious traditions; they exist, nevertheless, in partly disguised form in the central myths and theologies of many religions. We have learned not simply to flee, like St. Anthony in the desert, from these desires, but to take them seriously, indeed, to view them as revelatory. An existence that is so deeply unsatisfying that one's very biological organism cries out against it is revealed by that fact alone as needing change. This is not to say that deficiency needs are the only reality or that satisfying them willy-nilly is the only morally legitimate course of action. Deficiency needs must be considered in terms of a whole that includes many other structures and processes. But deficiency needs cannot just be dismissed or denied—they must be taken as one indication of the structure of reality.

The inner experience of fulfillment, not of need, has always been the chief "inner" dimension of transcendent reality. Herbert Richardson has recently argued that the chief aspects of such a religious experience are the feelings of wholeness, rightness, and well-being.[8] Unlike the experience of deficiency, the experience of fulfillment tends to overcome all oppositions, to be as much immanent as transcendent. Yet it is viewed subsequently as a revelation about reality, not simply as an aesthetic or emotional experience of a purely "subjective" sort. Such experiences are as basic in Western spirituality as in Asian religions. In Christianity one need think only of Paul on the road to Damascus, of Augustine in the garden in Milan, or of Luther, Pascal, Edwards, or Tillich to see that in different periods and with different theologies the experience itself has remained central. The categories of interpretation of the experience may of course differ significantly among various religions.

Abraham Maslow, in his analysis of what he calls "peak experiences," has pointed out that this experience of fulfillment is not confined to the conventionally religious sphere.[9] Individuals appear to have experiences analogous to the classical religious ones in the realms of love, art, sports, child rearing, and so on. To the extent that they are later interpreted as genuinely revelatory they are indeed parallel to religious experiences more narrowly defined. Let me turn to a particularly beautiful account in Stevens for an example of such "secular" revelation:

Perhaps

The truth depends on a walk around a lake,

A composing as the body tires, a stop
To see hepatica, a stop to watch
A definition growing certain and

A wait within that certainty, a rest
In the swags of pine-trees bordering the lake.

Perhaps there are times of inherent excellence,

As when the cock crows on the left and all
Is well, incalculable balances,
At which a kind of Swiss perfection comes

And a familiar music of the machine
Sets up its Schwärmerai, not balances
That we achieve but balances that happen,

As a man and woman meet and love forthwith.
Perhaps there are moments of awakening,
Extreme, fortuitous, personal, in which

We more than awaken, sit on the edge of sleep,
As on an elevation, and behold
The academies like structures in a mist.[10]

Elsewhere Stevens speaks of a moment when one experiences "A self that touches all edges."[11] It is curious that the notion of such experiences, being the exclusive property of religious virtuosi ever got started since these experiences are probably as old and as widespread as the human race itself. The present student generation seems to be particularly open to them and deeply affected by them.

The Social Factor

Without some such experience of Transcendence, consideration of the idea must probably remain abstract, verbal, and theoretical. Yet individual experience alone is an inadequate basis for knowledge of reality. Science proceeds on the assumption that experiments must be replicable, and indeed, scientific evidence is treated skeptically if it rests on the work of only one investigator and has not been replicated by others. Traditionally, religious men have acted on a parallel assumption. Individual religious experience must be checked against the experience of others. A religious tradition is really a community of religious experience. This is not to say that the religious experience of a community always takes precedence over an individual's when there is a conflict between them. But if an innovator fails to arouse any response from others, if others cannot participate in his new modes of experience, then his religious innovation dies with him and has no meaning for religious history.

Maslow has indicated the necessity of adequate social arrangements for dealing with deficiency needs as a prerequisite to personal growth toward self-realization. Religious experience of all kinds is almost impossible without some form of group support. Religious institutions are social settings for the encouragement of the spiritual life. When they seem no longer capable of fulfilling their function, revolutionary or reformist action to improve the situation also takes group form. Every great innovator has required his band of disciples and his lay sympathizers.

In a word, society is another locus for the confrontation with reality. In the work of Émile Durkheim society becomes almost the representative of a reality principle like Freud's. It is society, according to Durkheim, that disciplines the individual, raises him above his petty desires and interests, and supports his rational capacity to deal objectively with the structures of reality. Durkheim sees society not only as a hard taskmaster but as the source of the best in man, for it is only in and through society that one can be fully human. Perhaps Durkheim betrays his rabbinic heritage in that he holds not only that we should obey the law, but that it is worthy of our love.

It is through society that man encounters history; there is a historical dimension at the level of personality. But in society one's individual life history and history as collective experience intersect. History is the proving ground for both personal values and social values. Specific structures, personal and social, may prove inadequate in the face of the contingencies and catastrophes of history. In history reality is encountered as judgment, and no finite structure is ever entirely adequate to that encounter.

Since history reveals the inadequacy of every empirical society, it becomes clear that society can no more than the individual be a final repository of Transcendence. Every society is forced to appeal to some higher jurisdiction and to justify itself not entirely on its actual performance but through its commitment to unrealized goals or values. The kind of symbolism which societies develop to indicate their commitment to higher values and to define their legitimacy varies in historical perspective. But there is no society which can avoid such symbolism; it is necessary even in the most complex modern societies. Indeed, Herbert Richardson argues that it is especially necessary there:

> The total cybernetic system must be fortified by an eschatological symbolism which can provide it with general goals and assist men to make the continual transitions an increasingly complex system requires. A cybernetic system determines a rate and form of change, but it does not determine the ultimate end of change. Rather it is guided by some encompassing social vision of the good society. This vision cannot be conceptually precise—for then it would be static rather than dynamic. But it must be symbolically precise if it is to give real direction to the social process.
>
> The American philosopher Charles Peirce has helped us to understand the guiding power of a myth or symbol which must be conceptually "vague" if it is to guide rational development. Such a "vague" symbol is open to continual conceptual specification; hence it is capable of providing direction to a total cybernetic society. It is conceptually imprecise, but symbolically precise. Such symbolism must be religious, i.e., it must portray a transcendent kingdom of God. The very transcendent character of religious eschatology is the condition of its adequacy for guiding a cybernetic society; for trans-historical symbolism always retains the "vagueness" and conceptual openness that prevent man from expecting any absolute fulfillment in time. Only transcendent religious symbolism can undergird an infinite development of society at a controlled pace. Only "other-worldy" religious symbolism can preserve the system from falling into an intra-historical stasis.[12]

Symbols of Transcendence

Our analysis, then, forces us to consider the symbols which transcend individual and society, symbols which attempt to grasp reality as a whole, symbols like God, Being, Nothingness, and Life, that individuals and societies have used to make sense out of themselves and to give direction to their actions. These symbols may emerge out of individual, social, or historical experiences but they are not identical with those experiences. They are not symbols for empirical realities in any scientifically verifiable sense. In some respects they are systems of pure terminology, displaying what Kenneth Burke has called the principle of perfection that he finds inherent in language itself.[13] But these great summary symbols which refer to the totality of being, to the transcendent dimension of reality, and the differentiated terminologies which have grown up around them cannot be dismissed as "subjective" just because they are not in a simple sense "objective" in their reference. Transcendence symbols are neither objective nor subjective, neither cosmological nor psychological. Actually, they are relational symbols that are intended to overcome the dichotomies of ordinary conceptualization and bring together the whole of experience.

Now it seems clear to me that we cannot distinguish reality from our symbolizations of it. Being human, we can only think in symbols, only make sense of any experience in symbols. These considerations reopen the issue of a confrontation with reality conceived of as standing overagainst us. That formulation seems somehow to imply that we stand outside of reality, that there is a split between ourselves and reality. But that is not the case. We participate in reality, not passively but actively. Stevens, in another mood, can emphasize the openness of reality: "Reality is not what it is. It consists of the many realities which it can be made into."[14] Nowhere else is the creativity and openness of reality more apparent than in the realm of the highest, most comprehensive symbol systems themselves: "The world is the world through its theorists. Their function is to conceive of the whole and, from the center of their immense perspectives, to tell us about it."[15] This is the function of

> The impossible possible philosopher's man.
> The man who has had the time to think enough,
> The central man, the human globe, responsive
> As a mirror with a voice, the man of glass,
> Who in a million diamonds sums us up.[16]

The conclusion that Stevens drives toward is determined by his recognition of the nature of symbolism and of the kind of symbols that ultimate symbols are: "The final belief is to believe in a fiction, which you know to be a fiction, there being nothing else. The exquisite truth is to know that it is a fiction and that you believe in it willingly.[17]

It would be a mistake to think that this last quotation of Stevens cancels out all the others. For if he is the poet of the "Supreme Fiction" he remains also the poet of reality. Perhaps his position is best summed up in the line standing as a preface to this essay: "We believe without belief, beyond belief." Had he stopped with "We believe without belief," we might have understood him simply as a stoic existentialist trying to make the best of a world he never made. But "beyond belief " shows that the symbolism, unavoidable though it may be, is provisional, not final. "Central men" will go on giving us new conceptions of the whole that, though fictional and provisional, will take us ever deeper into the mystery of being.

Let me emphasize again that Stevens' is not a reductionistic theory of religious symbolism. It does not claim to explain religious symbolism as a simple function of biology, psychology, sociology, or history, though it involves all of them. Religious symbolism is necessitated by the inadequacy of all partial symbolisms. It has an irreducible *sui generis* nature. Without it man would not be human. We believe in it seriously, we believe in it willingly, we believe in it—if we follow Stevens—knowing it to be a fiction.

To press the issue one step further, it is the idiom of "belief " which forces us to the term "fiction." In important respects, however, religious symbolism operates differently from what we usually call belief. Stevens tells us that "The poem is the cry of its occasion,/ Part of the res itself and not about it."[18] Religious symbolization, too, is part of the religious experience itself and the experience would not be complete without its symbolization. Only when the symbol has been torn from its experiential context and taken literally as a belief "about" something must we assert its fictional nature. As part of the experience itself the symbol is perfectly and supremely real.

What seems to be a very "modern" theory of religious symbolism may be a necessary prerequisite for the adequate understanding of *any* religious symbolism, especially for the exacting task of understanding a symbol which is not one's own. In a recent book Wilfred Smith argues that to understand a religious symbol one

> . . . must ask oneself how much transcendence it can be made to carry for those who have chosen its particular shape to represent the pattern of their religiousness. The sacred must always be not only ambiguous but unlimited: it is a mystery, so that no specific significance can exhaust it—there is always more waiting to be explored. A religious symbol is successful if men can express in terms of it the highest and deepest vision of which they are capable, and if in terms of it that vision can be nourished and can be conveyed to others within one's group. . . . Admittedly, some progress towards understanding symbols can be made if one asks not what does the symbol mean, simply; but rather, what does it mean for the particular men who use it religiously. Fundamentally, however, even this must be transcended; one must think of the symbol in terms not of its meaning something, but of its focusing or crystallizing what *life* means, what the universe means, to those who through this symbol find that life and the universe can be seen (or felt) to *have* coherent meaning.[19]

One feature of this understanding of religious symbols derives from the fact that it views these symbols as final only provisionally, as ultimate not substantively but regulatively; this understanding is nonauthoritarian. The traditional view tended to make God an absolute or a benevolent despot. The postrevolutionary conception tends to make God into a democratic president who can be replaced at a later date by a more suitable candidate. One has by no means deprived the highest term of seriousness and authority. A democratic president must have authority and respect if he is to fulfill his function. But he is not immune to criticism. He exists in a reflexive, reticular relation to his electorate; communication is two-way. In considering the adequacy of any particular conceptualization of the whole, all the levels of consideration that I have developed above, and more, must be taken into account.

If, for instance, there is a conception of God that succeeds principally in producing anxiety in those who hold it and that exacerbates frustrated deficiency needs, then one may legitimately question the conception. Upon further consideration one may conclude that the social and historical situation is such that this conception of God is an adequate expression of godly reality—in which case what needs to be changed is not the conception of God but the social historical situation. But in principle no particular symbolization is itself above criticism.

A new feature of the modern situation is the extent to which it has become possible for everyone to appropriate religious symbol systems from many times and cultures. This variety has been made available to us through the achievements of historical and comparative research. Many different symbols can be appropriated if one views them as capable of "focusing or crystallizing what *life* means, what the universe means, to those who through this symbol find that life and the universe can be seen (or felt) to *have* coherent meaning." One can bracket one's other own symbolic commitments and see how another perspective would make life feel to *me*. One does that in a minor way any time one looks at a Chinese painting or listens to an Indian raga. It is only a step further to try to understand, with Nagarjuna, the absolute emptiness of the world or, with Chu Hsi, the organic network of interdependencies in the world. And it is only a step beyond that to recognize with Ernst Troeltsch that one's own religion is one's historical fate, but that that religion has no more claim to absoluteness or finality than any other. This is not to say that all religious symbol systems are of equal value and meaning, for clearly they are not, but rather that their relative meaning and value must be derived from their involvement in human existence, not from some transphysical fiat.

It might be asked whether religion might not be abandoned altogether once its symbolism is revealed as a supreme fiction. After all, the history of culture is the history of the growth of consciousness. Traditionally, religious symbolism has always been redolent of the unknown and the unconscious. As consciousness grows and ego more and more takes the place of id, cannot we expect the gradual disappearance of religious symbols?

The answer depends partly on one's definition of religion. It is true that a theory that recognizes the fictional quality of religious symbolism can no longer differentiate between religion and the highest and most serious forms of art (though it might be doubted whether in any definition of religion such forms of art can be entirely excluded). But the most serious issue has to do with whether the growth of consciousness itself can be expected to eliminate the need for religious symbols, the functions of Transcendence.

It seems worth arguing that the relation between consciousness and unconsciousness, between science and religion, is not of the nature of a zero sum so that more of one automatically guarantees less of the other. May it not be, as Philip Slater has suggested, that as the islands of consciousness grow broader the surrounding seas of the unconscious grow deeper? In any case, the need to integrate the whole, known and unknown, conscious and unconscious, grows stronger. Somehow or other men must have a sense of the whole. They must have something to believe in and to commit themselves to. Life in its immediacy will not yield to objective analysis, will not wait until all the research results are in. Men must act in the face of uncertainty and unpredictability and consequently they must have faith; they must be willing to take the gamble, the risk of faith. Symbolization of transcendent reality seems inescapable, whether religious in a traditional sense or not. Only transcendent symbolism can overcome the splits in consciousness—between public and private, individual and collective, conscious and unconscious, experience and concept, surrender and control—and so render personality, society, and culture capable of healthy activity.

Science itself posits an unknown, a mystery. If everything were grasped in terms of clear and distinct ideas, if everything were accurately predicted, there could be no *science*. Inquiry would be unnecessary. There would be no need of hypothesis, experiment, and verification. Instead there would be a kind of "paradise" in which "the boughs / Hang always heavy in that perfect sky, / Unchanging."[20] In such a paradise one would need neither science nor religion. Until that time, since both answer to the structure of human existence, both will continue.

This essay has been based on the assumption that the absolute separation of social science and theology is impossible. Every theology implies a sociology (and a psychology, and so on) and every sociology implies a theology. At least every definite theological position limits the variety of sociological positions compatible with it and vice versa. To say that sociology and theology are separate enterprises is neither to deny, as some have done, a relation between them nor to argue that they operate at levels so different that there is no necessity to integrate. On the contrary I would argue that theology and social science are parts of a single intellectual universe. To refuse to relate them is to admit intellectual bankruptcy; it is to admit an inability to confront the totality of human experience. I have much less confidence in the particular integration I have attempted than in a sense of the urgency of the task. With Stevens,

> We feel the obscurity of an order, a whole,
> A knowledge, that which arranged the rendezvous,
>
> Within its vital boundary, in the mind.
> We say God and the imagination are one . . .
> How high that highest candle lights the dark.
>
> Out of this same light, out of the central mind,
> We make a dwelling in the evening air,
> In which being there together is enough.[21]

REFERENCES

1. Wallace Stevens, *Collected Poems* (New York: Alfred A. Knopf, 1955), p. 336.
2. *Ibid.*, p. 383.
3. Wallace Stevens, *Opus Posthumous* (New York: Alfred A. Knopf, 1957), p. 238.
4. *Ibid.*, p. 237.
5. St. Augustine, *Confessions*, X.
6. St. Augustine, in Peter Brown, *Augustin of Hippo* (Berkeley: University of California Press, 1967), p. 405.
7. Abraham H. Maslow, *Toward a Psychology of Being* (New York: Van Nostrand, 1962), chapter 3.
8. Herbert W. Richardson, *Toward an American Theology* (New York: Harper & Row, 1967), chapter 3.
9. Maslow, *op. cit.*
10. Stevens, *Collected Poems, op. cit.*, p. 386.
11. *Ibid.*, p. 209.
12. Richardson, *op. cit.*, p. 24.
13. Kenneth Burke, *The Rhetoric of Religion* (Boston: Beacon Press, 1961).
14. Stevens, *Opus Posthumous, op. cit.*, p. 178.
15. *Ibid.*, p. 232.
16. Stevens, *Collected Poems, op. cit.*, p. 250.
17. Stevens, *Opus Posthumous, op. cit.*, p. 163.
18. Stevens, *Collected Poems, op. cit.*, p. 473.
19. Wilfred Cantwell Smith, *Problems of Religious Truth* (New York: Scribner's, 1967), pp. 16–17.
20. Stevens, *Collected Poems, op. cit.*, p. 69.
21. *Ibid.*, p. 524.

THREE MYTHS OF TRANSCENDENCE
HERBERT W. RICHARDSON

MODERN THEOLOGIANS TEND TOWARD CONSENSUS that an irreducible element in "true religion" is a certain feeling.[1]

There have, of course, been theological opponents of this position, e.g., Karl Barth and Emil Brunner. The opponents have not proposed an alternative interpretation of religious experience; they have proposed that theologians should choose an "objective revelation" manifest, for example, in the Bible or a historical tradition as their primary object of study, and should avoid entrapment in a "subjective experience." Even a theology based on scripture, however, must finally attempt to characterize the state of consciousness by which one experiences scripture as revelation. And even if religious experience is essentially a feeling, the experience need not be subjective, indescribable, and incommunicable since feeling in general is a perception and has a cognitive dimension. (By "feeling in general" I mean the irreducible, enduring state of consciousness which underlies and pervades the multiplicity of one's particular emotions, passions, or "feelings.")

In this essay I shall focus on the principal feeling that is constitutive of religious experience. First, however, a word on the anatomy of feeling. The concept of feeling can be clarified by defining an object of feeling, which is not like an object of seeing. An object of feeling is not like a tree, which can be denoted and denumerated "an individual." Rather, the object of feeling is a totality, or a whole, and an act of feeling is the perception of a whole.[2]

The theological consensus that defines religious experience as a feeling generally correlates the feeling itself with its proper "object," a whole. By the perception of a whole I mean the perception of a unit which is the context for a system of internal parts and their relations. Defense of the claim that a mere feeling can be a genuine experience of reality depends on a demonstration of the existence of a genuine object of feeling, of a whole. That demonstration of the reality of wholes has been twofold: (1) that they *are* experienced, and (2) that they are unitary and cannot, therefore, be conceived to be composites resulting from the mental act of combining parts of a system.[3]

The fact that a whole is not defined by its parts is the reason why wholes cannot be perceived by observation or made known by indication. It is this essential impossibility of denoting or denumerating wholes that encourages the specious contention that wholes are not really real. That wholes are not perceivable by ordinary observation does not mean that they are unreal; it means that they are not individual parts.

THE FEELING OF FEELING

Feeling perceives by participation. A whole is that which is perceived through participation. In the perception of a whole, the self takes up a position within the whole. The perception of wholes differs in this respect from the perception of individuals, for individuals can be observed and denoted from "outside." In observation, the perceiver and that which is perceived are not one. They stand in opposition to each other. But in feeling, the perceiver is one with the thing perceived. Thus feeling is a simple kind of consciousness "which involves no analysis, comparison, or any process whatsoever. . . ."[4]

In feeling, therefore, we perceive wholes by orienting ourselves *within* a gestalt that unifies both the ego and the ego's object. This gestalt is itself the whole that is the "object" of religious experience. For example, we feel "the immensity of the ocean" or "the presence of another." In these cases, the ocean's immensity and the other's presence seem to fill our consciousness so that we become one with them in communion. This communion, or feeling of wholeness, is a sense of direct participation in the reality of another. Hence, it "is the original expression of an *immediate* existence relationship.[5]

Thomas Kelly, a modern mystic, isolates just these characteristics in his description of the feeling of the presence of God:

The sense of Presence is as if two beings were joined in one single configuration, and the center of gravity is not in us but in that Other. As two bodies, closely attached together and whirling in the air, are predominantly determined by the heavier body, so does the sense of Presence carry within it a sense of our lives being in large part guided, dynamically moved from beyond our usual selves.[6]

Two other feelings generally accompany the feeling of wholeness, the feeling of rightness ("fittingness") and the feeling of well-being ("happiness").[7] The feeling of rightness is a perception of the rightness of things in general. This sense of rightness accompanies the feeling of wholeness because a whole determines a perspective from which certain individuals and relations that seemed at first to lack unity can now be perceived to be its parts. Such a general feeling of rightness is manifested in the "Aha experience," when we discern the unity of a multiplicity of parts within a gestalt. To use Ian Ramsey's expression for the moment of disclosure in a religious experience, this is when "the penny drops."[8]

The feeling of wholeness is also accompanied by a feeling of well-being ("happiness"), the feeling of being given what one wants, i.e., the feeling accompanying fulfillment.[9] When we are given what we want, we feel acknowledged by something more than ourselves. In a general feeling of well-being, we sense the tendency of all reality to fulfill what we desire and thereby to acknowledge our existence. When we have this feeling, we sense ourselves to be parts of a whole. The feeling of well-being, therefore, sustains self-esteem; and the lack of this feeling destroys it.

No states of consciousness are exclusively experiences of feeling. Our conscious experience is complex, involving a fusion of feeling perceptions, sensible observations, and symbolic relations; in certain experiences, however, one or another of these aspects seems to predominate. This is the case with religious experience. In religious experience, a person feels the All-Encompassing Whole. Because this feeling involves the participation of the subject, it is an experience of being part of the life of God.

Jonathan Edwards described this experience as follows:

. . . there came into my soul and was as it were diffused through it, a sense of the glory of the Divine Being; a new sense, quite different from any thing I ever experienced before. . . . I thought with myself, how excellent a Being that was, and how happy I should be, if I might enjoy that God, and be rapt up to him in heaven, and be as it were swallowed up in him forever![11]

Edwards' feeling of union with the All-Encompassing Whole was accompanied by the two other feelings we have discussed. It included feelings of the general rightness of all things ("how excellent a Being that was") and well-being ("how happy I should be, if I might enjoy that God, and be rapt up to him in heaven"). The feeling of union, then, is not identical with the sense of judgment (rightness) nor with a sense of personal salvation (well-being), though it is accompanied by these two feelings.

From these considerations, we can understand why religious experience has a transforming power and converts the subject to a new form of life. The feeling produced in a man by his participation in the Whole redirects his sense of rightness and well-being. With regard to the psychological and cognitive structure of such an experience, there is no difference between the transforming and elevating power of a finite whole and the power of the infinite Whole. Aesthetic feeling and religious feeling are similar in kind, though caused by different "objects" and encompassing different ranges of life.

MYTHS AND SIGNS

We should next consider how feelings of wholeness are communicated, for through such communication religious communities are formed.

For the sake of convenience, let us call all those symbols used to communicate religious experiences "images." Myths, archetypes, theological metaphors, and icons will then all be said to belong to the class of "images." They all belong to the same class of symbols because they all have the same foundation in the psychic life of man and embody the content they symbolize in the same manner. All these images symbolize wholes—though myth symbolizes the All-Encompassing Whole.

One must distinguish images from signs. Signs symbolize individuals; images symbolize wholes. Signs communicate by denotation, images by evocation. Signs are the means for communicating observations, images for communicating feeling experiences. Signs are external to the realities they signify (just as an observer is external to the object he observes); hence signs are conventional and replaceable. Images, on the other hand, participate in the reality they express (just as the subject participates in a whole by feeling); hence images are irreplaceable.

Without an image, a feeling experience is not only incommunicable but lost forever. If a feeling experience requires that its subject be included in and affected by the whole, then any whole is as transitory as the felt perception of it. Consider, for example, the moment when T. S. Eliot felt "the evening spread out against the sky as a patient etherized upon a table." That moment was a unique whole that included Eliot's feeling of it; without the poetic image it would have been lost. McLuhan was right in pointing out that "the medium is the message."[12]

The fact that the realities experienced in feeling are preserved only in images explains why images communicate not by naming but by evoking the reality they express. They can evoke this reality from themselves because they are expressive forms of it. A sign is not the expressive form of the individual that it names, but an image is the expressive form of the whole that it evokes. If we may take seriously the report of poets and prophets, then this expressive form is "given" by a whole to its perceiver—for it is the whole that affects him. Hence it is appropriate to say that the expressive symbol is "revealed" to the subject and he is "inspired" to receive it.[13] The act by which the poet or the prophet receives this revelation of the whole in an expressive symbol is an act of insight grounded in imagination. Such a view of imagination is different from the popular notion of imagination as a sheer act of creation in which one calls a fantasy world into being. But I suggest that the view set forth here is better able to account for the power of symbols to affect man and to transform and unify his life.

The status of images in this account is consistent with a number of statements in the contemporary theological and psychological "consensus": images participate in the reality they symbolize; images seem to exist independently of man—they are born and they die, and they cannot be created at will; images have the power to affect the lives of persons and to transform and integrate (or disintegrate) them; a special charisma is imputed to the creators and bearers of images and a special power to the images themselves.[14]

This complex of statements is consistent with the affirmation that images are revealed, or given, to man. The revelation-and-insight takes place only at a specific center which is the point at which the whole is constituted, since it is here that the whole and the individuals and relations which are its parts can be seen to intersect. In religions, the center is the "door" or "way" to life; it is the *kairos* or the *axis mundi*, ". . . the paradoxical place where [two worlds] communicate, where passage from the profane to the sacred world becomes possible."[15]

The first experience of the Whole at a specific center is only possible for one who discovers himself at this center. This is the prophet, who finds himself caught up in the Whole and whose utterance expresses his concrete feeling of it. Subsequent experiences of this Whole are possible for those who are affected by the prophet's utterance and feel the Whole as he felt it. A prophet's utterance does not simply evoke the Whole, but evokes the Whole as experienced from a specific center. Gerhard Lenski describes this phenomenon sociologically:

> . . . the theologies of most contemporary religious groups are more than trivia generated by contact with the hard realities of the current social situation. Rather, they are in large measure a heritage from the past, and at the very least reflect the exposure of past generations of believers to the social environment of earlier eras. . . . From this we might suppose that the theology of any religious association is the accumulated residue of responses to the social environment, both past and present. This gives us a closer approximation to reality, but when we get down to cases we discover the problem is even more complicated. If, for example, we examine the theological heritage of contemporary Mormonism, we discover that while it reflects the

influence of the frontier environment of nineteenth-century America, it reflects the influence of this environment *as it was experienced by Joseph Smith.* Whatever else we may say of Joseph Smith, he was no ordinary frontiersman of his day. Thus it is a matter of profound consequence that the environmental influences of the early nineteenth-century frontier on Mormonism were mediated through this unusual man.[16]

The prophet cannot be separated from his religious image, since this myth necessarily implies his mediatorial position at the *axis mundi.* One understands, then, that there can be no Christianity without Jesus Christ, no Mormonism without Joseph Smith, no Judaism without Moses. We can experience the Whole of which a prophet speaks only by joining him at the *axis mundi* and entering into his feeling of it. Thus, for example, Christianity asserts that we can experience the Whole only as we "take up the cross" and put on "the mind that was in Christ Jesus."

Since images create specific feelings in persons, there are genuine differences in religious experience from one religion to another. It is not correct to say that men who use different religious images all have the same religious feelings. Differences in religious images imply differences both in the feeling of wholeness and in the Wholes themselves. Hence, discernible differences in piety, spirituality, and feelings of virtue provide a basis for discriminating among religions with regard to the experience of God.

Religions are, in part, communities that are created and sustained by myths that form habitual modal feelings in the lives of their members. These habitual modal feelings are one of the bases for a religious communion among persons. While there may be private religious feeling which is not expressed in images, there can be no shared religious feeling without the use of religious images, or myths.

THREE MYTHS OF TRANSCENDENCE

The visual bias of our culture makes us susceptible to the assumption that images are visible symbols. But images may also be audible, tactile, or enactive. In fact, the primary vehicle of religious communication is mythic story and the ritual act.

The reason why the primary vehicle of religious communication is a myth, or "story-image," is because only thereby can the experienced whole be expressed as active, alive, and purposeful. Philosophical analysis—which by its very intellectual character tends to determine the ultimate as a concept—has never adequately refuted the criticism that it fails to do justice to a living God or a cosmic process. To do justice to ultimate reality as a purposeful life, one must experience it as a cosmic story that has a beginning, a middle, and an end.

We frequently fail to consider what this fact that myth is a story implies about the kind of meaning it has. The kind of meaning stories have is altogether different from the kind of meaning possessed by either naming words or sentences. Let us consider how this can be the case.

Language is not simply a collection of naming words. It is a complex unity of naming words joined into sentences that are joined into paragraphs that are joined into stories. Each of these linguistic units involves a different function of language and a different level of meaning. The meaning of a naming word comes from the thing it signifies. For this reason, naming words are conventional, replaceable signs. The word "man" can be replaced by the word "home" without any difference in meaning because both words draw their meaning from the object that they signify.

The meaning of a sentence, on the other hand, involves something more than the meaning of all the naming words it contains. Sentences unite naming words by using symbols that perform certain operations upon or establish certain relations among these naming words. Sentences may employ syntactical operators like "but," "whether," "and," "unimportant," and "greater than." Note that these words are not naming words; their meaning does not depend upon a sensible perception of either the external world or inner self-consciousness.

Sentences are also created by placing naming words in an order. The order adds something to the signification of the words it orders. It gives them a meaning as a sentence. Jerome S. Bruner, the Harvard psychologist, has provided an interesting illustration of this point. Suppose, he says, we give children the following table:

1	2	3	4	5
The	man	ate	his	lunch
A	lady	wore	my	hat
This	doctor	broke	a	bottle
My	son	drove	our	car

The children "soon discover that so long as they pick words in the order 1 2 3 4 5, from any place in each column, something 'sensible' can be got: even if it is silly or not true, like 'My doctor wore a car' or 'A lady ate a bottle,' it is at least not 'crazy' like 'Man the lunch his ate.' "[17] The experiment shows that a sentence has a meaning that is independent of the naming words it contains. Sentences may be "sensible" or meaningful on one level even if they are "silly" or not true on another. The same thing holds for mythical stories.

Just as the meaning of a sentence is more than that of all the naming words it contains, so the meaning of every story is more than that of all the sentences it contains. Thus we arrive at a third level of linguistic meaning, a level twice-removed from that of simple naming words.

We can understand the kind of meaning appropriate to stories by considering the following example. When children are in the first and second grades of school, they are given paragraph-long stories to read and are asked to suggest appropriate titles. They reply with a word or phrase or sentence: "Johnny takes a trip," "A surprise for Ruth," "Paul wins again," and so forth. The purpose of this exercise is to help the children grasp the meaning of the story as a whole. They are asked to see its "point." In so doing they come to understand how the meaning of the story is more than the meaning of all the words and all the sentences in the story. They show that they see the meaning of the story by summarizing it in· a title that is an image of the story taken as a whole. To utter this title, or image, evokes the whole story. It aims to express, in a shorthand way, "the instant vision of a complex process that ordinarily extends over a long period."[18]

We can carry this kind of analysis to a still more general level, however, and show not simply that every story has a titular unity, but that many apparently different stories deal with the same theme. Recall the tales of childhood: Hansel and Gretel, Cinderella, The Ugly Duckling, Peter Pan. The thematic structure of all these stories is that of the primitive Odyssey: separation and return. Their theme is the resolution of the crisis created by a person's separation from his true home, from the abode of his real identity and well-being.

The separation-and-return story is the primordial human myth. It reiterates the universal experience of birth (separation from the mother), the subsequent experience of feeding and being held (the fantasied return), and the anxieties created by the mother's (often displaced into the child's) coming and going. Stories dealing with this separation-and-return theme confirm for a child his primordial experience of the world; they help him to control his anxieties. The stories narratively "objectify" to him the feeling that his identity (his wholeness) is established in dependence upon the mother from whom he has been separated by birth, that his happiness is in returning to and being fed and held by her, and that it is right to call upon her and wrong to stray away from her (or to fear that she will stray away—that is, not be dependable). Such mythic stories communicate a certain feeling about the unity of life. They help a child to control his anxieties in the face of social and historical forces that rush him toward individuality and ultimate plurality.

Some childhood tales and games are thematically identical with the myths and rituals of primitive, prehistorical "nature religions." "Dust thou art," the saying goes, "and to dust thou shalt return." Or again, in the pietà statuary the mother from whose womb the Savior was born receives him back again (into her lap "womb"). Cyclical tales, based on the experience of primitive helplessness and total dependence upon a natural fate whose course one cannot control, provide fundamental answers to the cosmic question about the purpose and character of life. Their ritual and mythic thrust is seen in the fact that the process they describe is not simply told to but is formed in those who hear and enact (or play) them. In this way, primitive man (like the child) not only experiences the whole, but ritually has formed within himself religious feelings of wholeness, lightness, and happiness. He receives from the myth a total personal identity. His innermost feelings become expressive of a specific mythological orientation. That is, he is psychologically conformed to the theology of a mythic story. More exactly, the myth and his personal identity are experienced as "co-natural."

Because of the structural correspondence, or co-naturality, of mythic story and ritual person-forming acts, there is no such thing as a common experience of living transcendence. The primitive's or child's sense that he is nothing in himself and hence can exist only in total dependence on or by participation in the mother (or originating principle) is a specifiable and accurate description only of one kind of transcendence. It is an experience of transcendence rooted in man's sense of his own utter deficiency. It is an experience of God's compensating for what man can never be himself.

If "need" transcendence is given philosophical conceptualization, it will tend toward monism. God would be the absolute One, the sole real being. This is why an experience of this kind of transcendence can be attained, from adolescence onward, only by annihilating the psychological habits developed in order to individuate the ego and set it "overagainst" the world.

Because the process of individuation is so highly developed in Western society, both the separation-and-return myth and the monistic conception of transcendence are assumed by us to be "false." This is because Western men are formed psychologically by a different myth, the myth of conflict and vindication.

Although the Bible is filled with separation-and-return stories of children and men who stray from home or parents and fall upon difficulties from which they can be rescued only by return, it is more generally unified by the theme of conflict and vindication. This alternative myth was imposed upon the primitive odysseys, and conflict-and-vindication became the dominant worldview of the West. This myth has created new "outlookers" as well as a new outlook. It provides a different way to unify, identify, and regulate all life. The conflict-and-vindication myth makes Christianity and postprophetic Judaism historical and linear in contrast to the natural and cyclical separation-and-return religions that they displaced.

The conflict-and-vindication myth tells a story of man that comes from his being limited, oppressed, and suffering. Through a testing, man attains to the vindication of his personhood, his independent being. So, for example, archetypal Western stories are the bondage and exodus of Israel, the testing and triumph of David, the crucifixion and resurrection of Jesus, the martyrdom and glorification of the saints. All these stories inculcate a sense of reality as a structure of overagainstness experienced through conflict and formed in the person through his triumphal suffering.

The conflict-and-vindication myth, forming the sense of individuality in man, assists his growth away from absolute dependence upon the mother toward a condition of relative independence vis-à-vis a transcendent God. This development occurs, historically, with the emergence of biblical religion and Zoroastrianism. The movement of conflict-and-vindication life is no longer the cyclical death and rebirth, hunger and feeding, being lost and being found. It is, rather, a linear history of events aimed at a future goal, activated by a personal decision, social interaction, and faithful endurance. In this new myth, a man's identity is still established in relation to another—but now through overagainstness rather than through the participation characteristic of the separation-and-return orientation.

Though he is relatively independent, the conflict-and-vindication man cannot stand absolutely alone. He still needs to be in relation to another in order to affirm himself as independent. This may seem odd—for the fact of his continuing dependence on another (i.e., that he needs to define himself overagainst) is hidden from a person by the conflict through which he holds on to that other. The conflict is, therefore, ambivalent behavior manifesting both a desire for independence and a desire for dependence.

The conflict factor is essential to the establishment of personal identity. If we think, even today, about those we know who swallow the Jewish-Christian conflict-and-vindication myth whole, we may note the degree to which they need conflict and overagainstness in order to maintain their identity. The Jew needs the goy; the Christian needs the heretic.

The stage in psycho-social development that corresponds to the emergence of the conflict-and-vindication myth in biblical times is adolescence. Think, for example, about the conflict-and-vindication stories that fascinated us during our adolescent years: the radio serial heroes with whom we so identified—Jack Armstrong, Tom Mix, and the Lone Ranger. The television agonies of Batman, the Avengers, and the Man from U.N.C.L.E. similarly "turn on" our children. In all these tales the archetypal myth of conflict-and-vindication is given expression.

In conflict-and-vindication mythology, the hero triumphs not primarily because he is strong but because he is brave and good. The hero has to suffer to exhibit his worthiness. The goal of the conflict is not the destruction of one's enemy; it is one's *self*-vindication. From the conflict the hero gains an identity, an identity that is but the counterface of the enemy he opposes. He who fights Goliath is big because he fights something gigantic; he who faces SMERSH must be good because SMERSH is so very evil. This is why the young student protester must smash the WHOLE DAMN SYSTEM.

To win an identity through conflict, however, means that one is dependent upon that conflict to sustain the identity. Old soldiers, revolutionaries, and gridiron greats must actually or narratively reiterate the tale of their sufferings and triumphs. They are the counterface of their enemy.

The man who lives by the myth of conflict and vindication has, therefore, no positive identity; he is nothing in himself. He is fearful of those who would take away his enemy; he is suspicious of peace, disoriented by prosperity. What is most threatening to him is the lack of a war to be fought or work to be done. He must invent enemies to destroy and products to be worked for. To the extent that Christianity and Judaism inculcate the myth of conflict and vindication in a society of abundance (i.e., America), to that extent they underwrite and inculcate America's war and violence. To the extent that they inculcate the experience of transcendence as "over-againstness" and "other," to that extent they prop up the anxious person by encouraging him to project that which he fears within himself (his own negativity) outside himself. We justify our wars as "right," and throw ourselves into the yaw of death not in order to die but in order to find a meaning that can sustain our continual living. One must seriously ask whether Western society, which lives by the myth of conflict and vindication, can ever renounce war and violence.

In scarcity societies, the Jewish-Christian myth of conflict and vindication may be socially useful, for in scarcity societies real enemies threaten man on every side. In such a world "eating" is the opposite of "starving" and "work" is the alternative to "irresponsibility." But in a society of abundance, the necessities of life can be produced without work. To live in such a society requires, therefore, a positive identity. A man must possess the fullness of his being, his virtue, within himself. He must be his own thing.

What is needed today, therefore, is a new transcendence and identity myth as the foundation of the psycho-social order. There are signs that such a myth is emerging. Its theme is *integrity and transformation*. To illustrate it, let us compare the Greek odyssey of Homer with the vision of man's space odyssey in Kubrick's *2001: A Space Odyssey*.

The journeying of Ulysses takes him . . . home. But the odyssey of the space man takes him . . . nowhere. The end of his seeking is neither a place nor (given the infinity of space itself) is it a "conquest." That is, the end of the space man is not some "goal" in terms of which he either "cyclically" or "linearly" defines himself. It is, rather, his own self-transformation into a higher being, his spiritual rebirth, his divinization.

This rebirth (with which *2001* ends) is not from the maternity of a mother. It is the result of man's integrity to his own creative vision, to his own project for himself. By his integrity to this vision, man gains for himself his own positive identity, his own aseity of being. He no longer lives by dependence or obedience. He no longer lives by being "a part of" or "overagainst." He no longer needs another to complete him or compensate for his negativities. He can now live by what he is.

Conventionally speaking, the "integral" man has no needs at all—that is, he needs nothing outside himself in order to establish an identity or be happy. But the "integral" man may have another kind of need, namely the demand or requirement rooted in himself to be true to those tendencies that make him unique. To be "integral," then, is not to need to complete ourselves through others (or from "outside"), but to need to express and expand ourselves from within.

The kind of transcendence correlated with the myth of integrity and transformation is that of self-transcendence, expanded consciousness, spiritual rebirth, and divinization. In simplest terms, we may say that the "God" of integrity-and-transformation is not the one in whom we live (separation and return) or the one who limits and is overagainst us (conflict and vindication), but the one who lives in us. In our integrity we can experience transcendence as our own potentiality to become more, as the demand for self-transformation.

To speak of the completeness and sufficiency of every man does not mean that men shall become more isolated and separated from one another. It means the possibility of a new kind of human community. If, for example, I do not need another in order to complete my own identity, I can see the other for what he really is in himself rather than simply for what he is that correlates with my own needs. I can now love and affirm him as a unique friend.

Our social experience could then become multiplicative rather than just compensatory. Our consciousness could be "globalized" (Teilhard de Chardin) and we could live in "unimunity" (Ferré). In fact, whole societies could be regulated by cybernetics rather than by coercion, by the maximizing rather than by the minimizing of diversity.

REFERENCES

1. Basic works forming this consensus are Jonathan Edwards, *A Treatise Concerning Religious Affections*, Friedrich Schleiermacher, *On Religion*, Wilhelm Herrmann, *The Communion of the Christian with God . . .* , and Rudolf Otto, *The Idea of the Holy*, Stephan Strasser, *Das Gemüt*. For the history of this tradition see Leo Spitzer, *Classical and Christian Ideas of World Harmony*.
2. A defense of the distinction between individuals and wholes appears in my *Toward an American Theology* (New York: Harper & Row, 1967), Chapter IV.
3. We are bracketing "relations" from consideration since the notion of wholes can be attained through the contrast with individuals.
4. C. S. Peirce, *Collected Papers*, C. Hartshorne and P. Weiss, eds. (Cambridge, Mass., 1960), I, par. 306, p. 150.
5. Friedrich Schleiermacher, *Friedrich Schleiermachers sämmtliche Werke*, II/2, p. 586; cited in Richard Niebuhr, *Schleiermacher on Christ and Religion* (New York, 1964), p. 121.

6. Thomas Kelly, *A Testament of Devotion* (New York, 1941), p. 96.
7. The distinction is traditional. For example, Anselm speaks of *rectitudo* and *commodum*, Edwards of excellency and happiness, Ross of the right and the good.
8. Ian Ramsey uses this expression to indicate the moment of disclosure in a religious experience. The examples he gives are taken from gestalt psychology. See *Religious Language* (New York, 1963), pp. 22–30.
9. Happiness is, for example, when a little girl gets the doll she has "always wanted." She does not simply get a doll, she also gets a general sense that the world she lives in "cares" and will respond to her desires and her efforts. This sense of happiness is, therefore, a genuine feeling that life is successful. From such a feeling, a person is encouraged to try again, to move on. Abraham Maslow notes just this point when he writes: "Such experiences not only mean moving on, but have a feedback effect on the Self, in the feeling of certainty . . . self-trust, self-esteem." (*Toward a Psychology of Being* [New York, 1962], p. 55.) There are, in fact, certain "cosmic gifts" which engender a general sense of happiness; these are traditionally called "grace." Christianity should begin talking about grace much more forthrightly than it has in modern times—since this concept is necessary to an understanding of moral and intellectual growth.
10. From the metaphysical point of view, the feeling of rightness is the presupposition of the feeling of well-being; however, the two are so conjoined that they tend to be simultaneous in experience.
11. Jonathan Edwards, "Memoirs," *The Works of President Edwards* (New York, 1881), I, p. 16. Edwards' term "excellent" means "right." I have drawn heavily on Edwards' account of excellence in my description of rightness.
12. Marshall McLuhan, *Understanding Media: The Extensions of Man* (New York, 1965), Chapter I.
13. For example, Jacob Boehme's introductory sentences in his *Confessions* read as follows.
   Art has not wrote this, neither was there any time to consider how to set it punctually down, according to a right understanding of letters, but all was ordered to the direction of the Spirit, which often went in haste; so that in many words letters may be wanting, and in some places a capital letter for a word. . . . I can write nothing of myself but as a child which neither knows nor understands anything, which neither has ever been learnt; and I write only that which the Lord vouchsafes to know in me according to the measure as himself manifests in me.
14. For an example of such a "consensus" see the collection of essays in *Myth and Symbol*, F. Dillistone, ed. (London, 1965).
15. Mircea Eliade, *The Sacred and the Profane*, W. Trask, trans. (New York, 1961), p. 25.
16. Gerhard Lenski, *The Religious Factor* (New York, 1963), pp. 337f.
17. Jerome S. Bruner, *Toward a Theory of Instruction* (Cambridge, Mass.: Harvard University Press, 1966), pp. 78f.
18. McLuhan, *op. cit.*, p. 25.

ON THE MEANING OF "GOD": TRANSCENDENCE WITHOUT MYTHOLOGY

GORDON D. KAUFMAN

MANY HAVE OBSERVED that modern man, more than the man of any other age, lives in a world from which God is absent, a genuinely secular world. Our forefathers had a sense of God's continuous providential guidance of history as a whole and of their individual destinies in particular; they found their lives meaningful because they were lived within the context of God's purposes, each man having his own unique place and task. But such meaning as most men of our time find is the this-worldly humanly created meaning emergent from ordinary social intercourse and/or cultural activity. For some this loss of a transcendent source and purpose has reduced human life to meaninglessness and absurdity, a pointless and empty burden simply to be endured (Beckett); others react with bitterness and revulsion (Sartre); still others seem to find sufficient satisfaction in their daily round of activities, punctuated occasionally be aesthetic experience or unusual excitement, not to miss or lament the dimensions of depth and transcendence and mystery in which previous generations found their lives ensconced. But in any case the radical "eclipse of God" (Buber) or even the final irretrievable "death of God" (Nietzsche) appears to be the most momentous theological fact of our age. Given this cultural context, it is little wonder that linguistic analysts find it dubious whether the word "God" has any genuinely specifiable meaning,[1] and theological writers, in a desperate attempt to rescue the Christian faith from what appears to be its certain demise, seek wholly "secular" interpretations which go so far as to dispense with the word and idea of "God" entirely.[2]

I

The problem with the concept of "God" arises out of the fundamental metaphysical-cosmological dualism found in the Bible (as well as in traditional metaphysics) and in virtually all Western religious thought.[3] This is the division of reality into "earth" and "heaven"—that which is accessible to us in and through our experience and in some measure under our control, and that beyond our experience and not directly open to our knowledge or manipulation. The latter "world" is, if anything, more real and more significant than the experienced world, since it is God's own abiding place (from whence he directs the affairs of the cosmos) and man's ultimate home. In the Bible this dualism is expressed in full-blown mythological terms. Heaven is a kind of "place" or "world" in certain respects like the places found in the world of experience; it is peopled by "heavenly beings" and even a "heavenly court" visualized in analogy with earthly persons and political structures; and God is the absolute monarch ruling the cosmos in a way analogous to an Oriental despot.

Some writers, e.g., Bultmann, have supposed that if it were possible for Christian thinking to rid itself of this somewhat crude and unbelievable mythological machinery, faith in God would once more become a live option for contemporary man. But the difficulty is much deeper than that, for this elaborate and fantastic mythological imagery is simply a naive and embellished expression of a more fundamental problem: the religious presupposition of a reality other than or "beyond" this world, the assumption that *the eminent reality with which we have to do—God—is somehow "out there"* (or "up there" or "down there" or "in there"—it does not matter) *beyond the given realities of our experience.*

For the purposes of his "demythologizing" program Bultmann defines mythology as "the use of imagery to express the otherworldly in terms of this world and the divine in terms of human life, the other side in terms of this side."[4] But this leaves unquestioned the most problematic feature of mythological thinking: that there *is* an "otherworldly" or "other side" at all, which, in contrast with the "human," is to be viewed as "divine." Attempting to resolve the problem of myth by cutting away most of the minor mythological realities (demons, angels, and other supernatural and superpersonal powers), but continuing to speak of an "exalted Christ," of the "Word of God" as something which comes *to* man from some "beyond," and of "acts of God" which *transform* men and history, is to miss entirely the central problem posed by mythological language. For that problem does not arise from the mere picturing of another *world* ("heaven," "supernature") over against our world, in imagery drawn from within our world; the problem is whether there is *any significant reality at all* "above" or "beyond" or "below" the world which we know in our experience, or whether life is to be understood simply in this-worldly, i.e., secular, terms. Demythologizing which fails to come to terms with the ultimate metaphysical-cosmological dualism expressed in the mythology, and in fact at the root, of all Western religious thinking, is not seriously facing up to the problem of the irrelevance of Christian faith and the Christian church in contemporary life.

Men of other ages found it necessary to create and believe elaborate mythologies and metaphysics of the "beyond" in order to understand their world and themselves. Contemporary men in contrast—partially freed by scientific advance from the ignorance which mythological explanations attempted to fill, and through technological advance increasingly able to control forces which were to earlier generations simply mystery—find it more and more unnecessary and even ridiculous to make this dualistic assumption. They have learned in recent centuries that those claims to knowledge of reality which have warrant in this-worldly experience lead to prediction and control of their world, while speech about some "other world" or "supernatural reality" appears to be without warrant or significant effect, a merely traditional and probably superstitious usage.

The authority of church and Bible no longer suffices to sustain the dualistic position; indeed, it is precisely the dubiousness to many moderns of the metaphysical dualism which these "authorities" so unquestioningly take for granted that can be credited in part for their obviously waning significance in modern life. We seem thus faced with two options. The dualism can be given up without remainder as an unjustifiable metaphysical vestige from previous stages of civilization[5]—and it is difficult to see how anything recognizably Christian would remain if one took this course without some qualifications. Or else we must find a way in the present situation to restate (in terms not simply presupposing the old dualistic mythology) the contention that the ultimate reality with which man has to do is somehow "beyond" that which is directly given in experience. That is, we must seek to show in terms meaningful for our own time how it is possible and why it is significant to speak not only of this world but of "God." It is to this latter alternative that the present essay is directed.[6]

II

We may begin our investigation by asking about the purpose or intention of "God-language." What function does the word "God" perform in religious and theological speech? That is, which experiences or problems *in this world* seem to require some people to talk about extramundane reality? And why do they think such an odd extrapolation or postulation is necessary? When one puts the question this way, the first thing to be observed is that the question about God-language has been transformed from a strictly logical to a quasi-historical form. The problem to which we shall initially address ourselves is not the abstract and general problem of proving to any rational mind the meaningfulness and even truth of the concept of "God"; it is, rather, the concrete problem of locating the context and situation in which the word "God" is used and found appropriate and meaningful. Clearly, only if this latter task is performed first can the former be undertaken with any hope of significant outcome. Indeed, it may turn out that this word or its context has a peculiar character which makes impossible such general logical justification.

In connection with what sorts of questions or problems, then, has speech about God or another world emerged and been used? The answer is not far to seek. Such speech appears within the context of man's sense of limitation, finitude, guilt, and sin, on the one hand, and his question about the meaning or value or significance of himself, his life, and his world, on the other.[7]

On the one hand, man knows himself to be limited in many respects: God (or the gods, angels, demons, etc.) is seen as the reality which is the final limit to his being and power. This is the experiential dimension of the claim that God is creator, sovereign, lord of the world, and so forth: men experience themselves as "thrown" into a world (Heidegger) not of their own making and ultimately not under their control; they look forward to an end, death, which they may be able to defer slightly but which they can never avoid; they are hemmed in on all sides and determined by their peculiar aptitudes, temperaments, and interests, by the position in society and history into which they have been born, by circumstances of all sorts completely out of their control. The details of the analysis and elaboration of this awareness of limitation and weakness will of course differ widely in different cultures and traditions, and the way in which the limiting factor(s)—God—is understood will vary accordingly, but the basic *fact* of man's finiteness is rooted in man's actual situation as a particular limited being in the world.

When in the course of evolution man emerged to full consciousness and self-consciousness, it was inevitable that he would also become conscious of, and seek modes of interpretation of, this his finitude. The earliest forms of such interpretation were highly mythological and are no longer acceptable or meaningful to many moderns. But the problem which gave rise to those views remains, and talk about God in the contemporary context must be understood as a modern way of seeking to speak about these same issues. In this respect the idea of God functions as a *limiting concept,* i.e., a concept which does not primarily have content in its own right drawn directly out of a specific experience but which refers to that which we do *not* know but which is the ultimate limit of all our experiences. While ancient man spoke with some confidence in his knowledge of this reality *beyond the limits* of his world—and it is just this which makes his thought "mythological" or "gnostic," and dubious to many today—most moderns are somewhat more fastidious and restrict themselves to positive affirmation about only what falls *this side* of the limits.[8] But it must be observed that we, like ancient men, are also involved in a certain duality here, i.e., between what is in fact concretely experienced, and the limit(s) of all experience and knowledge.

On the other hand, as a being who lives in a world of symbolic meanings (i.e., who is a linguistic being) and values (i.e., who is a deciding and acting being, making choices between alternatives), man asks about the meaning and value of his own existence. His conscious experience and thought are made possible by his ability symbolically to compare and contrast the fragments and pieces of experience with each other through the creation of words and symbols and thus to build up a symbolical and ordered world of increasingly comprehensive wholes. His action in and measure of control over his world is made possible by his learning to create and define standards or criteria for evaluating alternatives before him, and his learning to discriminate with increasing precision between the realities of his experience in terms of these norms.

It is only natural, then, that he should ask about the meaning of his own existence within this structured world in which he finds himself, and the value of himself and his activity in the midst of all these other valued realities. This question becomes especially urgent in the light of his ultimate limitation and powerlessness, which seem to suggest that no lasting meaning or value can be placed on his being; certainly he by himself could not be its adequate source or ground. Once more, then, an answer to this question could be found only *beyond the limits* of human possibilities and knowledge.

Here again the mythologies of earlier generations were able to provide concrete answers. In the "other world," the world "beyond the grave," the inequities and injustices of this life are made right (doctrines of karma and the judgment of God, of heaven and of hell) and the value and meaning of human existence are assured. Though such affirmations could hardly be made simply on the basis of this-worldly experience, the religious myths provided a *gnosis* of the "beyond" (i.e., of God's nature and will, or of the ultimate order of things) which gave adequate assurance. In contrast, contemporary man finds it exceedingly difficult to speak with any confidence at all about that which is *beyond* the limits of his world, although the duality (between what is accessible to us and some ultimate limit) may be acknowledged.

It is in the context of these questions and problems about man's finitude and the significance of his existence in the light of this finitude that the meaning and use of the word "God" should be understood. That is, our speech about this Other arises because certain features of experience force us up against the limit(s) of all possible knowledge and experience. If there were no experiences within the world which brought us in this way up against the Limit of our world—if there were no point at which man sensed his finitude— then there would be no justification whatsoever for the use of "God-language."[9] This means that any persons (positivists?) who by temperament or training either do not often find themselves forced up against these limits, or do not choose to reflect on them when they are, will find speech about God seeming useless or empty.

Since it is in relation to this particular context of problems and experience and language that "God" has meaning or justifiable use, its significance or validity cannot be demonstrated to anyone who either refuses to acknowledge the legitimacy of the context or any substantial interest in it. In this sense, the problem of the meaning and importance of theological speech depends upon matters of temperament and history. But, though not everyone will acknowledge the significance of questions about the Limit, to those who do, such questions will appear to be of universal import; for every man (whether he acknowledges it or not and whether he is interested in this or not) stands under and within the limits here under consideration. It is not unimportant to raise the question, then, about the degree to which one's understanding of the issues here involved depends on the traditions which seem to him significant as well as the climactic historical occurrences in his own life.

III

We must now examine further the content of the term "God." Though the fact of ultimate limitations on our being and meaning provides the context within which religious language arises and has meaning, it is clear that more is intended by that language than simply the bare and abstract notion of Limit. It is not surprising that primitive man, in confronting this situation, created imagery (in analogy with certain concrete powers within his experience) by means of which the power of the ultimate Limit could be conceived; and so the mythological "other world" appeared as the home of the mysterious powers that invaded and controlled this world.

Our modern problem with theological language arises out of the fact that we no longer find it justifiable or meaningful to speak of this other world and the powers which inhabit it. Even when, in more sophisticated interpretations, the plethora of mythological powers supposedly controlling human destiny is reduced to one—God (or, as in a contemporary highly bloodless form, "being-itself ")—we are dubious of the claims to knowledge. And that for a rather obvious reason: if it is really the *limits* of our experience and knowledge with which we are here dealing, by what right can anyone speak of the nature or even the existence of reality beyond those limits? Here sheer agnosticism would seem to be not merely prudent but the only honest course as well.

Inasmuch as theological language often claims or pretends to speak of that *beyond* the limits of the humanly experienceable—even, upon occasion, claiming to know on the basis of "revelation" about the inner workings of the divine being(s)—it is not surprising that such talk seems highly dubious and even sheer nonsense to many. Limit means *limit*. And it is both deceitful and inconsistent on the one hand to justify talk about God on the ground of our limitedness, and then, on the other, to transcend those limits in order to spell out in some detail the structure of the reality that lies beyond them.

Insofar as theological language is involved in this sort of self-contradiction and self-delusion, it very rightly has fallen into ill repute. If the experiential base which justifies the very use of theological terms is man's awareness of his own finitude, then the fact of that finitude must be consistently adhered to in that language; and the too easy transcending of finitude implicit in every form of mythology must be renounced. Because the awareness of the "boundary situation" (Jaspers) within which man lives was first

expressed in mythological forms which themselves implicitly ig-
nored that boundary,[10] it has been extremely difficult to discern
clearly the experiential base which justifies theological language.
Consequently it has been supposed, both within the theological community and without, that theology deals primarily in
otherworldly realities. From this common assumption the religious
have proudly drawn the conclusion that they have been granted a
secret *gnosis* denied others, while the worldly supposed that theology dealt simply in old wives' tales and other superstitions about
some "other world" which the imagination of man has fabricated
out of whole cloth. Neither side was able to focus clearly on the
actual base *in concrete experience* from which theological work
proceeds, thus giving an interpretation of religious language which
could justify its use to contemporary secular man. It is clear that if
we have located correctly the experiential context of speech about
God, the theological vocabulary will have to be rebuilt from the
ground up with a much more sensitive ear to the epistemological
consequences *for theology itself* of the fundamental religious situation of limitedness.[11]

It is not possible to undertake that project in any detail in this
paper. The most that can be done is to analyze briefly the complex
character of the awareness of our finitude and the special
understanding of that awareness implicit in the use of the word
"God." It must be clear, of course, just what I am attempting here. I
am not seeking to develop a full-blown doctrine of God on the basis
of a kind of natural theology of human finitude. Rather, I am trying
to define with some precision the sort of "God-talk" which is justifiable and responsible from that base, as well as the limitations
which must be imposed on theological speech when one seeks to
avoid presupposing the traditional—and illegitimate! in the
modern view—mythology of two worlds. (If someone wishes to live
and speak within that mythological framework, of course that is his
business. I am here concerned with searching out the meaning
which theological language can have for those of us who no longer
find warrant for or meaning in that dualism.)

We begin then with a somewhat different duality than that of
two-world thinking: the duality of experience and its Limit(s). Such

content of the term "God" as derives from an alleged *gnosis* of some "other world," transmitted by mythological traditions, may not be admitted to consideration here, for our interest is in defining the meaning which the awareness of our finitude as such permits and requires.

IV

What kind of conception is this notion of ultimate Limit? Some existentialist literature seems to suggest that there is a particular immediate experience involved here which is to be contrasted with other experiences of lesser limits. I do not think this is a very careful reading of the matter. All that we ever experience directly are particular events of suffering, death (of others), joy, peace, and so on. It is only in *reflection upon these* and the attempt to *understand ourselves in the light of these happenings* that we become aware of our limitedness on all sides. Along with this awareness of our being hemmed in, powerful emotions of terror, despair, revulsion, anxiety, and the like, are often—perhaps always—generated, and this total intellectual-emotional complex may then be called the "experience of finitude" or awareness of the "boundary situation," or something of the sort. But it must be observed that this "experience" of radical contingency is not an *immediate* awareness of restriction, as when one butts one's head directly against a stone wall; it depends rather upon a generalization from such occasional immediate experiences of limitation to the total situation of the self.

The self, in this way perceived as hemmed in on all sides, comes to a new and deeper awareness of its nature and powers: it is *finite,* master neither of itself nor of its world. Thus, the so-called experience of finitude or contingency, however powerful the emotions which accompany and deepen and reinforce it, has an intellectual root, and it is possible only because man is a reflective being. (Dogs also die, but this does not lead them to despair over canine life, because they, presumably, are unable to anticipate their own death imaginatively and reflect on its meaning.) As we shall see below, the peculiar character of this complex experience—being rooted in particular simple experiences of restriction, but apprehended as referring to the contingency of the self (and of man generally) in every moment, man's boundedness on all sides—enables it to be the experiential ground both of theological conceptions and of nontheistic metaphysical schemas as well.

It is with the aid of concepts such as *limit* that the generalizing movement of consciousness from particular immediate experiences of restriction to the total situation of the self is made. This term, originally applying to physical boundary lines (e.g., between fields or nations), here becomes used metaphorically to designate the self's awareness of being circumscribed or hemmed in. How are such restriction and limitation to be conceived? The imagery built into the notion of limit by its physical origins reminds us that every *actual* limit or boundary which marks off and restricts *real being* (in contrast to, for example, a mathematical limit or similar abstract "limiting idea") must itself be conceived *as a reality, as having some kind of substance and structure.*[12] Thus, a city wall is made of earth and stones, a fence of wire and posts, and so forth. It is important to observe here, however, that only because we can examine the wall or fence from all sides, test it in various ways, and the like—that is, only because the limit is not an ultimate or absolute limit but can be surpassed—is it possible for us to know the stuff of which it consists. If we could not in any way *get beyond* the limit we were examining, we would have no means of directly discovering its nature but would have to construct the conception of it imaginatively out of elements more fully known in our experience.

Consider, for example, the situation of a man imprisoned in a cell outside of which he has never been and from which he absolutely cannot escape. If he seeks to conceive the restricting walls of his room—with their resistance to his efforts to push through them, their hardness and solidity and color—as (material) realities, he will be able to do so only in analogy with the experienceable (material) objects *within* the room. Thus, his conclusion that the walls are composed of some sort of *thickness* of material substance, however plausible, in fact presupposes an interpretation of that which is *beyond* what is directly experienceable by him, namely, the bare surface of the walls. The conception of the ultimate limit of his movements is constructed imaginatively out of elements derived from objects within his experience that partially restrict and limit him; for the stuff or structure of the walls themselves—that "behind" their surfaces—cannot be directly known, though the restrictingness of the walls is, of course, directly experienced.

The same point about the way in which the notion of the ultimate Limit is conceived by analogy with certain relative limits known within experience may be made with reference to another illustration, the ancient image of the "end of the world"—a kind of final edge of a bottomless abyss beyond which it is impossible to go. In this case it is obvious that what is *beyond the Limit* is being imagined rather precisely in terms of the intramundane experience of dangerous cliffs and other places from which one might fall to his destruction. Even the abstract notion of limit itself, we may now recall, was drawn originally from the experience of (relative) physical boundaries; only by analogical extension of its meaning could it be applied to the self in such a way that the sense of being completely circumscribed and confined—the awareness underlying the concept of finitude—could develop.[13] It is hardly surprising, then, that when we seek to conceive this Limit concretely, as restricting and constricting our actual being, images and notions drawn from concrete intramundane experiences of limitation provide the material making up the conception. Certain characteristics of known finite limits are abstracted from their context, and built by analogy into the notion of the ultimate Limit. Our problem, now, is to discern what experiences provide the images and what restrictions must be laid down governing their use in this way.

Let us recall what it is that is being limited here and see how its limits are in fact experienced. It is not property or a nation or even the world with which we are here concerned, but the self. The self's awareness of being restricted on all sides, rendering problematic the very meaning of its existence, gives rise to the question: *What* is it that in this way hems us in? How is this *ultimate* Limit, of which we are aware in the "experience of finitude," to be conceived? There appear to be four fundamental types of limiting experience, and these supply models with the aid of which the ultimate Limit can be conceived.

The first two are relatively simple: a) selves experience external *physical* limitation and restriction upon their activities through the resistance of material objects over against them; b) they experience from within the *organic* limitation of their own powers, especially in illness, weakness, failure, and exhaustion. The other two are somewhat more complex: c) they experience the external *personal* limitation of other selves engaged in activities and programs running counter to their own—i.e., the clash of wills, decisions, and purposes—but precisely because matters of volition and intention are subjective, this experience is neither simply internal nor external but is interpersonal and social; d) they experience the *normative* constraints and restrictions upon them expressed in such distinctions as true-false, real-illusory, good-bad, right-wrong, and beautiful-ugly, which distinctions, though felt subjectively and from within, appear to the self not to be its own spontaneous creations but to impinge upon it with categorical demands and claims.

The self is restricted in its actual willing and acting, in its formulation of projects and its attempts to actualize them, in each of these quite different ways. Each is the basis for a peculiar experience of the nature of limitation which cannot be reduced to any of the others. Thus, for example, it is not possible to understand the sense of being at cross purposes with and thus restricted by another person, in terms simply of the concept of *physical* resistance or limitation, any more than the experience of utter weakness in connection with a severe illness can be comprehended with categories derived from the concept of logical necessity.

Though these four modes of experienced limitation may sometimes be confused with each other and often (or perhaps always) are experienced in complex interconnection with each other, they are obviously distinct and separate. In each case the *limiter* is conceived in somewhat different terms so as to be appropriate to that of the self which is actually restricted. Thus, material objects impose physical restrictions, and physiological deficiencies limit our organic capacities; other active wills are responsible for personal constraints, while values and ideals impinge with normative force. In a situation such as imprisonment I experience physical restriction (the prison walls), but am also aware of the personal constraint of other wills (those who built the prison and put me in it), and perhaps of organic deterioration (increasing weakness due to poor food, lack of exercise, and such). Each restriction is involved with the others and with the concrete situation of imprisonment, and some (e.g., the physical restrictions) may be the result of others (the conflict of wills) and essential to the effective realization of those others; but none of the limiters can be reduced to any of the others. Escape from prison will not dissolve the conflict of wills, and personal reconciliation will not correct malnutrition. In each case the specific limiter restricting the self must be dealt with appropriately to its own nature.

If we turn now from this identification of the variety of finite limiters to the problem of understanding the ultimate Limit, it will be clear that there are a number of possibilities. The ultimate Limit could be understood on analogy with any one of the types of finite limiter, or through some combination of several of them; but there is no way of grasping the nature of the ultimate Limit simply and purely in its own terms. For, in the first place, if this is really the *Limit* beyond which we can never move at all, then by definition there could be no way for us directly to apprehend its character; at best we could experience and know its "surface," that is, its mere impingement as such, its limitingness, a quite abstract notion. But the ultimate Limit—being that which is apprehended as the *real* and *effective* restriction on our being and movement (no mere "empty idea")—is grasped as concrete actuality impinging on us, i.e., not merely abstractly but as having some concrete character or nature. Moreover, in the second place, as the preceding analysis has shown, awareness of the ultimate Limit is no fifth entirely distinct type of direct and immediate experience of limitation; on the contrary, this awareness arises only mediately through complex acts which generalize the immediate and particular experiences of constraints upon the self into the "experience of finitude."[14]

It is out of this complex experience that the question about an ultimate Limit over against the self first arises and it is within this context that any apprehension or conception of the ultimate Limit will emerge.[15] Insofar as its character or nature is explicitly conceived at all, it will evidently be understood then, with the aid of one or more of the actually experienced finite limiters (the experiences of which are the only concrete sorts of limitation we know), and will be interpreted in terms of implications derived from that (or those) image(s). Moreover, since there is no possible way to prove the special appropriateness of any one or combination of the finite limiters to perform this function (again, that would presuppose a direct knowledge of the nature of the absolute Limit, which, as we have seen, is not available), it is evident that any particular concrete conception of the ultimate Limit may be quite arbitrary.[16] Despite this difficulty we cannot avoid conceiving the Limit as concrete, for if it is apprehended at all, it must be apprehended as that which in fact constricts and constrains the actual concrete self.

Any of the types of finite limiter could serve as the model in terms of which a conception of the ultimate Limit might be developed, but difficulties arise when any one of them is used exclusively. Thus, when physical limitation is taken as the fundamental analogy, a materialistic worldview results and man's being is understood as simply a function of the physical universe. This is a common enough view and has much to commend it, notably the obvious dependence of all man's functions on his physical being. However, it is very difficult to see how the other types of limiter are to be understood simply in physical terms. This problem is often dealt with in modern times through some conception of emergent evolution, but the problems here are immense and probably insoluble for a purely materialistic point of view. Hence one may be led, as with Whitehead or Bergson, to seek a resolution of the difficulties with some sort of organicism or vitalism. Yet it is difficult to see how the notion of organic limitation is really of much help in developing a conception of the world which does justice to the other limiters. Similar problems arise with the various forms of idealism which take normative limitation to be the most fundamental.

However, our objective here is not to resolve these difficult problems of metaphysics but rather to examine the grounds for speech about God when the traditional mythological dualism is given up.

The ultimate experiential ground for such speech should now be evident. Talk about God appears when the ultimate Limit is understood on analogy with the experience of *personal limiting* as known in the intercourse and interaction of personal wills. In this respect religious faith opts for one particular metaphysical alternative from among the several available. However, this metaphysical decision is not of mere speculative interest, for the option involved is active will, that over against which a self can live in interaction and intercourse and communion. The other options understand the ultimate Limit in terms of an image of dead being or passive structure (as a quasi-physical limiter or like certain aspects of a normative limiter), or else as a vital but unconscious and certainly purposeless force (like an organic limiter and/or certain other features of a normative limiter). Though each of these significantly interprets certain dimensions of our experience, none of them comes directly to grips with our distinctive experience as persons in communities, as conscious, active, deciding, purposing beings living in a symbolical world which provides the context and the possibility for continuous communication and intercourse with others.

The interpretation of the ultimate Limit in terms of this social level and dimension of our experience—which, however dependent it may be on the others in many respects, is the presupposition of our having any experience (properly so called)—is the metaphysical prerogative of theistic religion and defines its peculiar character. The religious attractiveness of this metaphysics—in that the ultimate context of human existence is here seen as personal and purposive volitional activity and not dead matter or unfeeling logical structure or unconscious vital power—makes theism relevant to the existential problems of the person in a way unmatched by any of the other metaphysical alternatives.[17] Hence, it very naturally appears as the essential ideological dimension of most religious faith. But precisely this same attractiveness makes theistic belief seem so dubious to many, in that the powerful desire of man to find genuine purpose and meaning in his life here seems too easily and happily fulfilled. The intrinsic anthropomorphism of this perspective thus makes it at once suspect and seductive. (This, of course, really does not bear directly on the question of its actual truth, since *all* the metaphysical alternatives conceive the ultimate Limit with the aid of a more or less arbitrarily chosen finite model.)

V

When a personal limiter is the analogical basis for understanding the ultimate Limit, a doctrine of God results. The ultimate Limit is then conceived in quasi-personal terms to be understood most decisively with notions drawn originally from the language used to deal with interpersonal experience. It is clear that this conception is the one operative in the biblical tradition where God is spoken of as lord, father, judge, king, and so on, and he is said to love and hate, to make covenants with his people, to perform "mighty acts," to be characterized by mercy, forgiveness, faithfulness, patience, wisdom, and the like—all terms drawn from the linguistic region of interpersonal discourse. Moreover, the biblical God is understood not to be accessible to man's every beck and call; he is not some structure or reality immanent in human experience and thus directly available to man. On the contrary, he resides in lofty transcendence, whence he acts in complete freedom to change the course of history or to reveal himself to his people through his prophets.

Now it is clear that this image of inaccessible transcendence and freedom made known and effective through explicit acts of communication and power—through words and deeds—is built up analogically from the model of the hiddenness and transcendence and freedom of the finite self, who also can (in some significant measure) hide himself from his fellows and remain inaccessible, except as he chooses to manifest himself through acts and words.[18] Though other terminology and images are also found in the biblical materials, there can be no doubt that personalistic language and conceptions most decisively shape the biblical view of the ultimate Limit.

I contended earlier in this paper, however, that the biblical and Christian traditions appear determined in large part by a metaphysical-cosmological dualism characteristic of mythology and no longer meaningful to many moderns. Moreover, it has often been held that precisely the anthropomorphic image of God as personal is an especially crude example of the mythological thinking of primitive man and therefore to be regarded as only symbolic or picture language, of significance in worship or prayer but not adequate for precise theological or philosophical work. We must now ask, therefore, how far a personalistic conception of God is essentially bound up with an inadequate mythology, how far it may be an independent and justifiable interpretation of the ultimate Limit.

It should be evident that to conceive the ultimate Limit personalistically is formally neither more nor less mythological than to conceive it on analogy with any of the other types of finite limiter. Each has its own peculiar appropriateness to certain dimensions of the self's experience of limitation, and each has difficulty in interpreting the other dimensions. With respect to the experience of limitation itself, then, no reason for preferring any of the four to the others can be given.[19] Moreover, inasmuch as it is necessary to grasp the ultimate Limit in terms of *some* model if it is to be adequately conceived at all, the attempt to grasp it personalistically should not be rejected as mythological (in the dubious sense of claiming unwarranted knowledge of that *beyond* the Limit) in any way not also applicable to every other attempt to apprehend and understand our finitude.

In a manner not characteristic of the other finite limiters, however, the personalistic image lends itself to a reopening of the question not only of the Limit, but of what is beyond it. For (as we noted above) it interprets man's relationship to that which ultimately limits him as being like his relationship to the finite selves with which he is in interaction. Such selves over against me always transcend in their subjectivity and freedom what is directly accessible to me in my experience (i.e., their bodies) even though they "come to me" and communicate with me in and through this physical dimension of their being that is open to my view. What I directly experience of the other, strictly speaking, are the external physical sights and sounds which he makes, not the deciding, acting, purposing center of the self—though I have no doubt these externalities are not *merely* physical phenomena but are the outward and visible expression of inner thought, purpose, intention. Thus I do not speak merely of "sights and sounds" but of the "sights and sounds which *he* makes" in *his* attempt to act or to communicate.

In my interaction with other persons I presuppose a reality (the active center of the self) *beyond* that which I immediately perceive, a reality encountered by me and known to me not simply in physiologically-based perception (though that is of course also involved) but in and through the language which we jointly speak.[20] It is in the act of communication that we discover that the other is more than merely physical being, is a conscious self; it is in the experience of speaking and hearing that we come to know the *personal* hidden behind and in the merely physical.[21] This is the most powerful experience we have of *transcendence of the given* on the finite level, the awareness of genuine activity and reality *beyond* and *behind* what is directly open to our view.

When this type of complex interrelationship is used to interpret the ultimate Limit, it is clear that an active reality (or "self ") beyond the Limit—beyond what is directly experienceable as such—will be implied. A self in its active center is never directly open to view, but is known only as he reveals himself in communication and communion. Likewise, on this model God cannot be identified with what is accessible to or within our experience, not even with the ultimate Limit of our experience; rather this Limit must be grasped as the *medium* through which God encounters us (as noises and gestures are media for finite selves), God himself being conceived as the dynamic acting reality beyond the Limit.[22]

In this way a certain reference to reality beyond the Limit of our experience is intrinsic to the personalistic image, and therefore such reference need not depend upon nor involve a reversion to mythology. It must be emphasized, however, that reference of this sort to transcendent reality is justifiable only when the ultimate Limit is understood in terms of a personal limiter; for only in the interaction with other selves do we encounter an active reality which comes to us from beyond what is accessible in experience. Organic, physical, and normative limiters can all be interpreted exhaustively in terms of what is given in and to experience (though it is not essential to do so), and it is mythology, therefore, if one speaks of a transcendent extra-experiential reality on the basis of one of those models; a personal limiter alone necessarily and intrinsically involves genuine transcendence.[23]

Correlative with this reference to a locus of reality beyond the Limit there must be a conception of revelation. We know the transcendent reality of other selves only as they act toward and communicate with us, as they reveal to us their reality and character and purposes in word and deed. So also, only if we are prepared to acknowledge some genuine encounter with God through his own actions directed toward us, is it appropriate to speak of the ultimate Limit in personalistic terms, i.e., with "God-language." By definition we could know nothing of any personal being beyond the Limit of our experience if that being did not in some way manifest himself to us through our experience or its Limit.[24] Once again, the organic, physical, and normative analogies for understanding the ultimate Limit require no doctrine of revelation, nor is any appropriate to them. This is the mode of knowledge characteristic of interpersonal communion, and it is when such encounters are taken as the model for understanding the Limit of all experience that the category of revelation is required.[25] Thus, to speak of God acting or God revealing himself is not necessarily to make a mythological statement presupposing an unjustified and unjustifiable metaphysical-cosmological dualism; such forms of conceptualization and speech are necessary if and whenever a personal limiter is taken as the model for grasping the ultimate Limit.

VI

Most attempts to locate the experiential referent or basis for the term "God" heretofore have accepted the framework of what I here called metaphysical or mythological dualism and then tried to justify in terms of some sort of direct "experience of God," or "apprehension of the infinite," or something similar. For those who had such experiences or intuitions, these analyses doubtless had meaning and significance; but for others of a more secular or this-worldly temperament or turn of mind, this seemed to be nothing more than paying rather extravagant "metaphysical compliments" to certain dimensions of experience.

The present analysis does not rest on the assumed validity of some esoteric experience of the other world or the supernatural or even the "numinous" (Otto). On the contrary, I have claimed that the experiential root of the notion of God is simply the awareness of Limit or finitude (known in some form by every man). In and of itself this awareness does not presuppose or imply some "infinite" or "unconditional" being. Indeed, only when it is grasped and interpreted in concrete personalistic terms does the Limit become understood as the expression of a being transcending our world, i.e., of an active God.[26] Thus, the constitutive *experience* underlying the word "God" is that of limitation; the constitutive *image* which gives the term its peculiar transcendent reference is personalistic. These fused into one in the concretely religious apprehension of our finitude provide us with the root referent for the word.

This double rootage accounts for the fact that, on the one hand, the presence or action of God is sometimes said to be immediately "experienced" or "known," and, accordingly, doctrines of religious experience are developed. On the other hand, it is often maintained that the knowledge of God rests on "faith" or "belief," and that he cannot be experienced directly at all. If, as I am arguing, the most we could be said to experience directly here is our bare finitude as such—and even this is a very complex sort of "experience" which is never apprehended concretely apart from the image of one or another of the finite limiters used analogically—then the truth in both claims can be understood: the encounter with God will involve both the "experience" of our finitude and the faith-interpretation through which this limitedness is apprehended as due to an active will over against us.

Since in the actual encounter with God these two elements so interpenetrate each other as not to be separately distinguishable,[27] there is little wonder that conflicting views about the relative importance of "experience" and "faith" appear. The faith interpretation, of course, is shaped by the concrete historical tradition within which one stands. If one stands within the Christian tradition, which knows of a loving and powerful Creator, it is hardly surprising that he will tend to see the course and destiny of his own being—i.e., its limits on all sides—as determined by the activity of

God: God's mercy and benevolence toward him will be felt in that which seems good in life; his·judgment and wrath, in the painful and constrictive.[28]

I conclude, therefore, that God-language is not necessarily hopelessly mythological and old-fashioned, but that, if carefully defined and restricted, it has a genuine basis in our awareness and knowledge of the Limit. This of course does not mean that the door is opened wide again for the well-structured "other world" of much traditional Christian thought. We have found it possible and legitimate to speak only of the reality which ultimately limits us on all sides—i.e., God—in this way. Of the existence beyond the Limit of finite beings alongside God—angels, demons, supernatural powers of all sorts, or the departed spirits of the dead—we know nothing and can know nothing.

There is no warrant in the present analysis, then, for reintroducing the "mythological worldview" in any form at all.[29] Since historically Christian theology grew out of and accepted rather uncritically the cosmological dualism underlying and expressed in that worldview, and in many details seems still to presuppose it, it is necessary to think through the whole of the Christian perspective afresh, sifting out all mythological elements to arrive at what of Christian faith modern, this-worldly man can affirm. Only when this winnowing has been performed will we be in a position to see whether the essentials of Christian belief in fact depend on the acceptance of a mythology meaningless and even ridiculous to moderns, or whether Christian faith can be a live issue in our secular culture.

I have tried in this paper to show that there is some justification for continuing to speak of a personal God even though the mythological framework characteristic of earlier speech of this sort be completely given up. This of course in no way can or should be construed as a kind of proof of the existence of such a God. As we have seen, there are other ways of conceiving the ultimate Limit which may in some respects seem more credible. All that I have attempted here is to show that "God-language" has its roots in concrete (secular) experience and that its cognitive meaningfulness can be defended, even granting the premises of "secular man"; whether it is *true* or not is another question. Our analysis has brought us into a position from which we can see what would be required if the truth of this claim were to be affirmed, however. Only on the ground that God had in fact revealed himself could it be claimed he exists; only if there were and is some sort of movement from beyond the Limit to us, making known to us through the medium of the Limit the reality of that which lies beyond, could we be in a position to speak of such reality at all; only if God actually "spoke" to man could we know there is a God. It is of course the Christian claim that God has acted to reveal himself and continues to do so. Whether that claim is true or not—and the grounds on which one might decide its truth—cannot be taken up in this paper; a full systematic theology would be required to deal with it. This paper should have made clear, however, that genuine knowledge of God could not be affirmed on any other basis than such revelation, and that the Christian claim is, therefore, directly relevant to the general philosophical question of God's existence.

REFERENCES

1. For a summary of the discussion see F. Ferré, *Language, Logic and God* (New York: Harper, 1961), and also W. T. Blackstone, *The Problem of Religious Knowledge* (Englewood Cliffs, N. J.: Prentice-Hall, 1963).
2. Cf. e.g., Paul Van Buren, *The Secular Meaning of the Gospel* (New York: Macmillan, 1963).
3. Karl Barth, who supposed himself not to be engaged in metaphysical or cosmological "speculations," nevertheless made a considerable point of the essential duality of the world in the Christian view. Cf. *Church Dogmatics* (Edinburgh: T. & T. Clark, 1936–1962). III /1, pp. 17ff.; III /3, pp. 369ff.; etc.
4. *Kerygma and Myth,* ed. H. W. Bartsch (London: S.P.C.K., 1953), p. 10, n. 2.
5. Auguste Comte more than a century ago, of course, already took this position, and he has proved to be the prophet of modern man in this respect.
6. It should be observed that the present essay is concerned with the question of the *meaning* rather than the *truth* of statements containing the word "God." No attempt will be made here to prove either that God does or does not exist, that is, that the word "God" does or does not actually refer to a reality. Questions of that sort can be faced only if we already know what we mean when we use the word "God"—the issue to which this essay is directed. (It should be evident that—certain "neo-orthodox" theologians to the contrary notwithstanding—prior discussion of the meaning of "God" is just as important for "Christian faith" as for "philosophy of religion," for it is meaningless to speak of "what God has done" or "what God has revealed" if it is doubtful whether the word "God" itself has any referential meaning.) It is my contention that the underlying assumption both of theists and atheists is that

"God-language" *presupposes* the validity of what I have above called the mythological-cosmological dualism between this world and another world, the holy and the secular, the eternal and the temporal, the absolute and the relative. Believers find themselves defending one or another of the several forms of this dualism; unbelievers (as well as many believers, if the truth be admitted) find the whole dualistic conception without sufficient warrant and possibly even a ludicrous vestige of earlier stages of culture. The question of the meaning and significance of speaking about God at all thus tends to get decided not in its own terms but on the basis of a prior attitude taken up toward the dualism of this world and the other. The purpose of this essay is to show that the meaning of the word "God," even in its reference to the "transcendent," can be developed and understood entirely in terms of this-worldly (i.e., secular) experiences and conceptions—that is, in terms fully comprehensible and significant to the most "modern" of men—and that therefore the whole issue of a presupposed cosmological dualism, so problematic for modern man, can be bypassed. In English the word "God" is understood by some to designate a mere psychological projection of a father-image and by others to indicate the Father of Jesus Christ and the ultimate reality with which we have to do. Since we are here attempting to uncover the basis on which significant conversation between such diverse points of view may proceed, and are not trying to prejudice the case for one or the other of these alternatives, it is evident that our delineation of meaning will need to have great flexibility. Doubtless to believers the present analysis may seem to concede too much to psychological reductionism; to unbelievers, too much to outgrown superstition. However, my intention is to favor neither view—that would be to argue the question of *truth* not *meaning*—but to provide a framework of meaning within which each can take up his position and arguments without prejudice, and within which, therefore, genuinely significant conversation between them can once again proceed.

7. The emphases of biblical faith on salvation, deliverance, succor, abundant life, forgiveness, resurrection, atonement, eternal life, etc., all have this double reference, negatively to man's inadequacy and need and positively to man's meaningful destiny and fulfillment.

8. In this respect modern man appears to be more heir of the skeptical than the metaphysical tradition in philosophy. One remembers, for example, the speech of Hume's Philo at the end of Part 8 of the *Dialogues Concerning Natural Religion:*
   All religious systems, it is confessed, are subject to great and insuperable difficulties. Each disputant triumphs in his turn, while he carries on an offensive war, and exposes the absurdities, barbarities, and pernicious tenets of his antagonist. But all of them, on the whole, prepare a complete triumph for the *sceptic,* who tells them that no system ought ever to be assented to with regard to any subject. A total suspense of judgment is here our only reasonable resource. And if every attack, as is commonly observed, and no defense among theologians is successful, how complete must be *his* victory who remains always, with all mankind, on the offensive, and has himself no fixed station or abiding city which he is ever, on any occasion, obliged to defend?

9. The highly complex character of this "experience" of finitude will be briefly analyzed in section IV.

10. It may be observed in passing that, despite all his strictures to the contrary,

Jaspers also really allows his alleged "boundary situations" to be surpassable under certain circumstances in the experience of what he calls "transcendence" (see, e.g., *Philosophie* [Berlin: Springer Verlag, 1948, 2nd ed.], pp. 44ff., 470, 675ff.). In the respect and degree to which this is the case his conception and analysis of finitude represent one more attempt to deny its real meaning, and my more drastic interpretation of the "boundary situation" should not be confused with his. (For similar criticism of Jaspers, see also Karl Barth's analysis in *Church Dogmatics*, III /2, pp. 109–121.)

11. It goes without saying that my repeated use of such terms as "finite," "limit," etc., is meant simply to *characterize* man; the respects in which man's finitude might be either "good" or "evil" is not considered. The usage is intended as neutral description.

12. I do not think the notion of a mathematical limit, which is always approached asymptotically but never actually reached, can serve as a root conception for the notion of *metaphysical limit* with which we are here working. For the awareness of finitude is not purely conceptual or hypothetical; it is an awareness of *my actual being* as here (in this time and place) rather than there, as restricted in this particular concrete way by aptitudes, interests, and training, as one that must and shall in fact die. It is the awareness of *my being limited* that we are here dealing with and thus in some sense an actual "encounter" with that which *limits me*. The notion of an asymptotic approach to a limit is simply not applicable, and we must revert to the physical experiences of limitation for models for our concept.

13. In view of this complex structure of the concept of limit—it being derived from the experience of relative limits which can be surpassed, and then extended to the notion of ultimate Limit which cannot—we should really not be surprised that men of all ages have supposed they actually knew something of that beyond the Limit, and that they expressed this in what I have above designated as mythological thinking. The duality of conscious finite being and Limit very easily, and almost naturally, goes over into the dualism of this world and the other world. These facts also throw light on the roots and meaning of Kant's first antinomy.

14. It will be observed that, though in many respects my position resembles Schleiermacher's, at this point I am setting myself against his contention that we have a specific and unique sense of absolute dependence as such (cf., *The Christian Faith* [Edinburgh: T. & T. Clark, 1928], § 3–5).

15. It might be helpful to summarize here the various phases of the complex process through which, according to this analysis, the conception of an ultimate Limit is formulated: (1) there must be particular concrete experiences of limitation (of the several types described); (2) the self must be sufficiently mature and reflective to be able to move from consciousness of these particular experiences to a more general concept of limitation or finitude; (3) the awareness of the significance that it is *I* who am in this inescapable way hemmed in must arise, together with the powerful emotions which contribute to the "experience of finitude"; (4) this awareness of my own radical contingency may then give rise to the question about *what* it is which so confines and limits me; (5) the ultimate Limit may then be conceived in terms of one (or possibly some combination) of the four types of finite limiter. It should not be thought that the complexity of this process in any way prejudices the legitimacy of the question (4) or the possible truth of the answer (5). For it is

certainly conceivable that we are limited ultimately by some (one) reality, and, if so, that only through some such complex process could we—all our knowledge being rooted in experiences of the finite—come to know it. As we shall see, if the ultimate Limit were personal (as the notion of "God" suggests), we would expect him to be known through complex mediatorial processes in any case (as is a finite person), and there would seem to be no reason why these processes could not include the sort here suggested (cf. reference 25). On the other hand, it must also be admitted that there seems to be no compelling necessity to move from step (3) in the above process through (4) and (5). One could claim (positivistically), if one chose to do so, that the only *what* which limits me are the four types of finite limiter as experienced in (1), and that there is no reason to suppose there is some one reality beyond and behind these which is the *ultimate Limiter*. The fact that the present analysis of the consciousness of finitude lends itself to such varied sorts of interpretation is no shortcoming; it means, rather, that significantly different perspectives—from positivism to a variety of types of metaphysics and Christian theology—can enter into common discourse with the aid of this framework, and this is precisely what we are seeking to make possible with this analysis (see reference 6).

16. It is, of course, better that we be aware of these peculiar difficulties in the conception with which we are dealing here than, in ignorance, simply refuse to face the question at all. In this respect Kant, who saw that we could never resolve the antinomies and problems of metaphysics but who also saw that we could never cease struggling with these issues (see, e.g., *The Critique of Pure Reason,* A849/B877–A851/B879), was much wiser than many of his latter-day (positivistic, existentialistic, and fideistic) followers.

17. If in this essay I were seeking an argument for the truth of theism, instead of limiting myself to an analysis of the experiential bases for—and thus the root meaning of—the word "God," it would be necessary and appropriate to expand and develop some of the implications of these sentences (see also reference 19).

18. For a full discussion of this claim that genuine transcendence is intrinsically a personalistic notion and can be consistently developed only in connection with a personalistic conception of God, see my paper on "Two Models of Transcendence," in *The Heritage of Christian Thought, Essays in Honor of Robert L. Calhoun,* ed. R. E. Cushman and E. Grislis (New York: Harper & Row, 1965).

19. It might be noted here, however, that inasmuch as the personalistic model involves the notion of a self whose active center is *beyond* that which is directly experienced, the latter being conceived as the vehicle or medium of the self's action or revelation, there is a certain flexibility and breadth in theism enabling it to deal with the considerable diversity of types of finite limiter somewhat more easily, perhaps, than can other kinds of metaphysics.

20. To avoid confusion in this already very complex analysis, I shall use the term "encounter" to designate the linguistic-experiential ground of our knowledge of other selves, reserving the more general term "experience" for the sensory-perceptual foundations of our knowledge of physical objects (including the bodies of persons *qua* their purely physical character).

21. For a more linguistically oriented treatment of these problems which comes to

fundamentally similar conclusions on the basis of careful analysis of personalistic modes of speech, see Stuart Hampshire, *Thought and Action* (New York: Viking Press, 1960).

22. In an early paper Paul Tillich seemed to be taking a position close to the analysis of this essay. "The non-symbolic element in all religious knowledge is the experience of the unconditioned as the boundary, ground, and abyss of everything conditioned. This experience is the boundary-experience of human reason and therefore expressible in negative-rational terms. But the unconditioned is not God. God is the affirmative concept pointing beyond the boundary of the negative-rational terms and therefore itself a positive-symbolic term" ("Symbol and Knowledge," *Journal of Liberal Religion* [1940], II, p. 203). Tillich, however, failed to refine his analysis and develop his insight. Thus, the peculiar character of "boundary experiences" remains unanalyzed here, and the "boundary" can even be interpreted in terms of such positive images as the (almost hypostatized) "unconditioned" or "ground"; this blurs its radical character as the ultimate unsurpassable Limit. Again (similar to my analysis), "God" is distinguished from "the unconditioned" as "a positive-symbolic term" pointing beyond the ultimate boundary, but Tillich fails to see (either here or anywhere else in his writings) that this is because of the peculiar character of the transcendence known only in interpersonal relations and is thus intrinsically connected with the personalistic overtones of the term "God." In his later writings, where Tillich apparently gives up the view that the "non-symbolic element in all religious knowledge" is a special experience and holds instead that we can make at least one nonsymbolic *statement* about God (see, e.g., *Systematic Theology* [Chicago: University of Chicago Press, 1951], I, pp. 238ff.), there remains little resemblance to the view I am trying to develop in the present essay.

23. For further discussion, see my paper cited in reference 18.

24. Since, according to the present analysis, every *positive* doctrine of God must rest on revelation, it should be clear both (a) why no real doctrine of God appears here (no concrete revelation being expounded), and (b) that the present analysis of "limit" is not to be confused with the "negative way" *to* God.

25. It will be observed that, according to the analysis presented here, the "encounter" with God actually rests on a double mediation, whereas our encounters with finite selves involve only the single mediation (of noises, visible gestures, etc.) discussed in the text: (a) the ultimate Limit is not immediately experienced, but is known only through the mediation provided by reflection on and generalization of particular experiences of limitation (cf. reference 15); (b) the "selfhood" or "nature" of God is not immediately experienced or directly encountered, but is known through the mediation of the ultimate Limit. This does not mean, however, that an "encounter" with God is really the product of a rather long chain of somewhat dubious inferences and no encounter with a reality at all. Rather, as the encounter with other selves makes clear, such communication through media is the mode in which realities transcending the reach of our immediate experience are known to us. In such an encounter, of course, I do not attend directly to the mediating processes (the noises the other is making); rather, I am conscious of *him*, of the speaker. Insofar as I must attend to his *words*, consciously, in bewilderment

about their meaning, making deliberate inferences, the process of communication is halting and ineffective. Only if I can and do "leap beyond" the media to the self who is mediated through these words is there significant encounter with the other. In most of our intercourse with others precisely this leap is made in the most natural fashion; this is why we say we *know* the other *person,* and not merely the noises he makes. In a similar way, God is never directly "experienced," but is "encountered" (as is appropriate to his transcendence) only in and through media. (The *double* mediation involved in this case, in contrast with finite selves, is appropriate to the fact that this is *God,* and not merely some intramundane reality, of whom we are here speaking.) If the media are the focus of attention here, of course the encounter with God will seem problematic and unreal; as with a finite self, only if and when a "leap beyond" the media (although through the media) occurs will the encounter with God be felt as genuine, i.e., only then could one properly speak of *God* being encountered. Theologically such moments are referred to as "revelation," i.e. God's self-manifestation. It is only because men have believed these to have occurred to themselves, or others, that talk about "encounters" with God—and thus talk about "God"—has appeared and continues to be sustained in human discourse. *Faith,* we can now see, is that stance in which the "experience" of the ultimate Limit is apprehended as the medium of the encounter with God (see section VI); *unfaith* is that attitude which, unable to "leap beyond" the ultimate Limit, finds itself always attending instead to the mere Limit as such.

26. It might be argued that it is no accident that such impersonal philosophical notions as "infinite" or "unconditional" reality, "being itself," the bare notion of "transcendence," etc., appear always as demythologized or depersonalized versions of the more anthropomorphic god(s) of a religious tradition, and that in their impersonal (sometimes called "superpersonal") form they are in fact denying the vital root on which their very life and meaning depend.

27. See reference 25.

28. If we have correctly identified the experiental elements underlying the term "God," the doctrine of God must always deal in some fashion with the notion of transcendent reality (even if only to refer it to some "depth" in everything that is) and with the way in which this transcendence is known to us (i.e., with "revelation"). However, such highly problematic negative notions as "infinite" and "unconditional"—probably rooted ultimately in "mystical" experience of the "supernatural"—would perhaps not need to be given the constitutive role in a doctrine of God which they have so often played in the past (though they might well have a certain secondary and interpretative role to play); and the meaning of the doctrine would not in that way be placed so completely out of reach of those whose direct experience seems to them limited to the finite and contingent.

29. It should perhaps be observed that my contention that such a doctrine of God would not be mythological rests on a distinction between "mythological" and "analogical." A *mythological* doctrine of God *begins in* and *presupposes* what I have called the cosmological dualism of "this world" and "another world," "this side" and "the other side." For such a presupposition there seems little warrant. An *analogical* doctrine of God makes no such presupposition, but results when (the experience of) finitude is understood in personalistic terms.

Thus, an analogical doctrine, being experientially rooted, can be carefully disciplined and controlled methodologically; with mythology the rootage is so vague and legendary that strict methodological control is almost impossible. For the position I am taking here, only if the Christian *doctrine of God* itself—worked out in strict accord with the foundations of theological knowledge as sketched in this essay—were to require the reintroduction of certain features of the otherwise discarded mythical world view, would it be justifiable to reinstate them. But this is as it should be: Christian faith is first of all faith in *God*—and all else that must be said theologically should follow from this premise.

TRANSCENDENCE IN CONTEMPORARY CULTURE: PHILOSOPHICAL REFLECTIONS AND A JEWISH TESTIMONY

EMIL L. FACKENHEIM

TRANSCENDENCE IN THE MODERN WORLD

APPEARANCES SUGGEST that the modern world has lost Transcendence beyond all possible recovery. No avenue seems left.

The Greeks contemplated nature and sought first causes. The modern scientist seeks mere uniformities, and his purpose with nature is not the contemplation of it but rather control over it. But who will find—or even seek—Transcendence in what he controls? Some may still find Transcendence in nature where it is uncontrollable and certainly as yet uncontrolled. Yet such is even now the effect of technology on contemporary culture that henceforth any such recourse to nature is destined to be judged not as an access to Transcendence, but rather as a flight from immanence. And the flight is in vain.

The picture is no different for consciousness within than for nature without. Mystics of all times and all places have found Transcendence within the soul, when in a moment of ecstasy it "stands outside itself," touched by an Infinity beyond it. In the modern world, however, mystical experiences are a rarity, and, more importantly, distrusted even when they occur. The pale cast of psychological and sociological thought has reduced what was once "Reality" to a mere feeling projected on reality, thus destroying the feeling itself. And, whatever the present limitations of psychological and sociological reflection, such is its hold on contemporary culture even now as to make every purported mystical access to the infinite Self seem in truth to be a mere flight from the finite self. And the flight is as vain when it is into a long lost mythical past as when it occurs in a chemically induced present.

What of the avenue to Transcendence most characteristically associated with the Western world? This is neither nature-contemplation, which has had no real home in the West since ancient times, nor mysticism, whose home is more in the Eastern than in the Western world. Since biblical times, the Western, Judeo-Christian world has found Transcendence in history. This has happened for better: in the midst of the human-historical world was found a Transcendence other-than-human and higher-than-human which gave meaning, if not to all of history, so at any rate to crucial, epoch-making events within it. Perhaps it has happened also for worse, for at least to non-Western minds it must often seem that the West lays a greater burden on history than it can bear.

Transcendence in history, too, seems to have vanished. Biblical man heard a commanding and promising divine Voice, and he perceived divine salvation with his own eyes. Modern man has reduced all divine to human voices, for whether inspired by Kant or Dewey, Nietzsche or Marx, he has "transvalued" divine commandments into manmade "values," and transformed promises to be redeemed by God into hopes to be realized by man. As for saving acts of divine Presence, perceived in moments of radical surprise when the unexpected and unexpectable become actual,[1] modern man has lost radical surprise, and treats unexpected and unexpectable events either as subject to explanation after all, or else as the product of chance.

Such is the consensus concerning Transcendence in our modern, technological, secular civilization. It is shallow at least when it is certain of itself and takes itself to be conclusive, and it is more rather than less shallow when it derives this certainty concerning present and future from scientific evidence. The voice of God is rarely heard in scientific generalizations, and is apt to confound scientific predictions. The cautious social scientist is well advised to confine himself to the short-range future. As for the wise historian, he never plays prophet anyhow.

The philosopher, too, is well advised to exercise caution. Part of his native equipment, philosophical caution is never more apposite than on the accessibility of Transcendence, and never more so than when the temptation is to make a priori assertions concerning it.

Throughout history men have found access to Transcendence in the most varied ways. Is it likely that they were, one and all, simply deluded—and that with very little effort a priori rational or linguistic analysis can now disclose what has all along been the truth? What if any truth thus arrived at were at best only a twentieth-century truth? What if the human condition presupposed, described, or postulated by logical positivism, linguistic empiricism, and atheistic existentialism were merely a modern-secularist condition and the philosophies describing it nothing more than a reflection of that condition? Long ago Hegel said that philosophy cannot transcend its time.[2] In the crisis of the present age, might not a philosopher match the historian's caution and refuse to play prophet?

Hegel himself compared the modern crisis to that of late Roman antiquity. Were he alive today (when the crisis already evident at his time has advanced much further) he might have perceived both much closer analogies and a much greater need to refrain from predictions, prophecies, and even any except the most cautious sociological generalizations. In the Roman pantheon the gods were all assembled and, because they had been made subservient to human use, they were demythologized and destroyed. Sociologists might have predicted that there could be no new gods, while theologians might have prophesied that all the gods had died. All this might have happened. Yet Christianity was just about to conquer the Western world.

The above, Hegelian-style reflections are themselves in the biblical tradition in that they suggest the possibility that Transcendence, rather than accessible either always or not at all, may differ in its accessibility according to historical circumstances. Such a view raises at all times the immediate question as to how, in any given historical here-and-now, Transcendence may be authenticated. In an age such as the present one (when access to Transcendence seems lost), it raises the additional question of how there can be any authentication of its very possibility. The second question can be answered at once. There can be no authentication if access to Transcendence is either a mere memory or a mere hope. A past which can no longer be reenacted and a future which cannot yet be anticipated are mere flights from present reality. An age that is one of "eclipse of God" (Buber), or that is "too late for the gods and too early for being" (Heidegger), can be recognized for what it is only if there is divine revelation in the divine self-concealment itself.

What of the first question? Authentication is possible only by a witness who *exists in* his particular situation, not by scientific observers, philosophers, or theologians who fancy themselves as transcending every all-too-particular situation. Public-opinion polls, conducted in the waning days of the Roman Empire, would have corroborated the pagan despair of the gods and dismissed Jews and Christians as oddballs and cranks. Similar polls, conducted in the Middle Ages, would have confirmed Christianity, but in so doing subscribed to the assumptions of Constantinian imperialism. One can be witness to a Transcendence which transcends the historical situation only *within* one's historical situation; nor can others who could appraise or respond to this testimony do so except from within *their* historical situation. There is no impartial, independent vantage point. But as for the objective uncertainty and the historical existential limitations bound up with this state of affairs, these are, so far as men's relation to Transcendence is concerned, boundaries which they cannot escape. In a unique situation, a witness or group of witnesses can never be quite certain that Transcendence speaks to them, and they must always be open to the possibility that it speaks differently to others.

Yet there are at least negative criteria by which claims to authenticity may and must be appraised. Neither Jewish nor Christian witnesses could have survived the collapse of the Roman Empire had they failed to satisfy two conditions. The God of Israel and the church, who had already proved to be unassimilable to the Roman pantheon while its gods were still alive, had to be capable of surviving their death, thus being a God of the present and the future as well as of the past. And He had to be a God commanding not idle curiosity or passing fancy, but faithfulness unto death. An anachronistic god could not have been kept alive even by the blood of martyrs; and even the most up-to-date god is not a living God unless He can raise up witnesses, however few in number, who are faithful unto death.

The question which arises in the present age is therefore as follows: *Can there be, in the present age, ways of testimony to Transcendence which, on the one hand, are totally present, contemporary and nonanachronistic and which, on the other hand, are not idle fancies or abstract conceits, but are forced on men or groups of men in their contemporary condition and by that condition so as to command absolute loyalty?*

With this question, a Jewish philosopher's reflection *about* the present general situation must necessarily turn into a Jewish testimony from within his present particular Jewish situation. This would be true in any age. It is truer in this age than in almost all others. For Jews of this generation have been singled out by the Nazi holocaust as Jews have not been singled out since the events at Mount Sinai.

THE VOICE AT AUSCHWITZ

The Nazi holocaust is totally present, contemporary, and nonanachronistic. The passage of time has brought it closer rather than moving it farther away, disclosing that the world has thus far shied away from it but must at length confront it with an unyielding realism and, if necessary, despair.

A secular liberalism which celebrates the loss of Transcendence in the modern world would dismiss the holocaust as a mere lapse into atavistic tribalism. This is but one of many ways in which attempts have been made to avoid the stark contemporaneity of its horror. Others making such attempts include Christian theologians ignoring the implications of the fact that the holocaust occurred in Christian (or post-Christian) Europe, Germans who disconnect it with the remainder of German history, and communists who cover it with the blanket term "fascism," and who bury fascism itself in the Marxist dialectic. Historians too disregard the holocaust—or, if they do not ignore it, they find it hard to return from it to their normal business.

Secularist-liberal ideology is not wholly blind to the fact that the blessings of the secular city are ambiguous. The anonymity produced by the fragmentation of communal ties alienates as well as liberates. The Promethean power provided by modern technology has destructive as well as constructive potentialities. The freedom from a premodern religious oppressiveness permits the permissible —and suggests that all things are permitted. Secularist-liberal ideology can face these ambiguities so long as it can ignore their demonic possibilities, pretending that the demonic is a mere species of "prejudice and superstition," safely destroyed by modern enlightenment.[3]

The Nazi holocaust destroys this pretense. Nazi antisemitism was not "prejudice," but a groundless, infinite, and implacable hate. Nazi racism was not "superstition," but mass murder infused with infinite passion and elevated to pseudoreligious absoluteness, not a finite means to the winning of a war, but a boundless end in itself, pursued even at the risk of losing a war on account of it. Dethroning all gods ever worshiped anywhere, Nazism assumed the vacated throne in order to presume to decide what peoples had a right to live and what peoples did not. And the decision was both made and executed in a terrifyingly contemporary framework. For the first time in history, murder became an industry whose products included human hair and soap made of human bodies. An ancient Midrash asks what became of the fear of God when the Romans destroyed Jerusalem, and it answers that it is because this fear still exists that Israel, now scattered helpless among the nations, is not destroyed by them. After Auschwitz, this answer has become impossible.

The Nazi holocaust hurls at all contemporary mankind the demonic assertion that if there is no God, everything is permitted. No contemporary man—secularist or religious—can ignore that challenge. We cannot say that Nazism is safely past; the world still gives Hitler posthumous victories. Nor can we say that it affects only its immediate victims. When the bomb fell on Hiroshima (and not into the sea), and when a shot killed Martin Luther King in Memphis, or, for that matter, when Gomulka stirred Polish antisemitism against the pitifully few survivors of the Nazi slaughter, Hitler must have laughed in hell.

In May 1967, the worldwide Jewish community had a moment of truth which revealed clearly, if only momentarily, what has remained otherwise obscure and ambiguous, or even wholly concealed. Jewish students dropped their studies and rushed to Israel. Elderly gentlemen of modest means mortgaged their homes. Tactful Jewish spokesmen abandoned tact and screamed, at the risk of alienating Christian friends. Faced with the fact that the state of Israel was in mortal danger, the worldwide Jewish community became, for a moment, wholly united in its defense. More precisely, time-honored divisions—between orthodox and liberal, Zionist and non-Zionist, religious and secularist—lost for a time their significance, to be replaced by a new division between Jews willing to stand up and be counted, and Jews who (whatever their reasons, excuses, or ideologies) stood aside.

What caused this unexpected and unprecedented response to an unexpected and unprecedented situation? Not "nationalism"; among those standing up to be counted were non-Zionists and even anti-Zionists. Not "religious sentiment"; the response transcended all religious-secularist distinctions. Not "humanism"; not a few Jewish humanists stood aside when Jewish—rather than Arab or Vietnamese—children were in danger. The true cause cannot be in doubt. For a whole generation Jews had lived with the Nazi holocaust, racked by grief and true or imagined guilt. For a whole generation they had not known how to live with the fact that Jews had been singled out for murder by one part of the world and that the other part had done little to stop it. When in May 1967 the same words issued from Cairo and Damascus that had once issued from Berlin, Jews were divided not into orthodox and liberal, religious and secularist, Zionist and non-Zionist, but into those who fled (and were revealed as having fled all along) from being singled out by the first holocaust and those who responded to it (and were revealed as having responded all along) with a resolve that there must be no second holocaust.

In what terms shall we understand this response? Much too puny are all categories which do justice to but relative commitments such as group loyalty or the "values" of a half-remembered tradition. Indeed, *all* past categories are inadequate, even when they do justice to absolute commitments, if only because religious categories exclude the secular, and secularist categories, the religious. Nothing less will do than to say that *a commanding Voice speaks from Ausch-witz; that some Jews hear it while others stop their ears; and that among Jews hearing it are secularists who hear no more and believ-ers who identify its Source.* No redeeming Voice is heard, or ever will be heard, at Auschwitz. *But Transcendence is found at Ausch-witz in the form of absolute Command.*[4]

JEWISH SURVIVAL

What does the Voice at Auschwitz command? In a recent, pre-six-day-war symposium on Jewish Values in the Post-Holocaust Future I replied: "The authentic Jew of today is forbidden to hand Hitler yet another posthumous victory." This commandment I specified as follows:

> We are, first, commanded to survive as Jews, lest the Jewish people perish. We are commanded, second, to remember in our very guts and bones the martyrs of the holocaust, lest their memory perish. We are forbidden, thirdly, to deny or despair of God, however much we may have to contend with Him or with belief in Him, lest Judaism perish. We are forbidden, finally, to despair of the world as the place which is to become the Kingdom of God, lest we help make it a meaningless place in which God is dead or irrelevant and everything is permitted. To abandon any of these imperatives, in response to Hitler's victory at Auschwitz, would be to hand him yet other, post-humous victories.[5]

Even as I wrote these words I realized their fragmentariness and their temporariness. Jewish survival is a duty, and indeed after Auschwitz, in itself a monumental act of faith; yet it is not, as it never has been, an ultimate end in itself. Jews may not despair of the world, but after Auschwitz they know no longer—and not yet—how to hope for it. Jews may not deny the God of Israel, yet after Auschwitz even many believers know no longer—and not yet—how to affirm Him. We must remember the martyrs of Ausch-witz; but we cannot yet do so without remembering Hitler along with them. Jewish tradition, however, would require that his name be wiped out rather than remembered, for to remember him forever would give him a victory forever, leaving the earth defiled and unhealed.

Since Auschwitz, Jews are singled out by an evil at once wholly demonic and wholly modern. They can survive as Jews only if they accept rather than flee from this singled-out condition, transfiguring victimization by the modern demons concentrated at Auschwitz into testimony against them everywhere. But they will have the strength for such testimony only if they hear the commanding Voice of Auschwitz. Like Israel in June 1967, the Jewish people as a whole will be saved by "the commandment which the Lord of history [has] . . . , so to speak, pronounced at Auschwitz."[6]

When the Roman world waned ancient paganism perished, but Judaism was renewed and Christianity originated. Is our modern crisis as radical as the ancient one? Is our question, too, what will perish and what will be renewed or transfigured? In the age of Auschwitz, Hiroshima, and the shot that rang at Memphis, perhaps Transcendence speaks to us all primordially through the Voice of Command. Perhaps to have any hope for renewal we must listen to that Voice, lest the demons unleashed by a mechanizing age destroy us.

It may be objected that in a postreligious, secular age, one cannot hear such a Voice. But perhaps our crisis is far deeper than is generally imagined in that secularity, as well as religiosity, is in question. And perhaps we shall all be saved by a commanding Voice which can be heard by secularists as well as believers, revealing to both, and most clearly so in the places of the most extreme human degradation, that man is created in the divine image.[7]

REFERENCES

1. For the notion of radical surprise here referred to, see my "Man and His World in the Perspective of Judaism: Reflections on Expo '67," *Judaism*, Spring 1967; Reprinted in *New Theology No. 5* (New York: Macmillan, 1968).

2. For the understanding of Hegel reflected in this essay, see my *The Religious Dimension in Hegel's Thought* (Bloomington: Indiana University Press, 1968).

3. I have developed the criticism here merely hinted at much more fully in "Possibilities of Idolatry in the Modern World," in *The Religious Situation: 1968*, Donald R. Cutler, ed. (Boston: Beacon Press, 1968).

4. Long after the ideas of this section were conceived, but before the words were put down, I received a letter from Professor Harold Fisch of Bar-Ilan University, Israel, which reads in part as follows:
   May I report to you a conversation I had last summer with a colleague, a psychologist, who had served during the war as an artillery officer in Sinai. I

asked him how he accounted for the remarkable heroism of the quite ordinary soldier of the line, for, as you may know, exemplary heroism was the
normal thing at that time; mere carrying out of duty was the exception.
Where, I asked him, was the psychological spring? To my surprise, he
answered that what deeply motivated each and every soldier was the
memory of the holocaust, and the feeling that *above all this must never
happen again.* There had been an ominous similarity between the statements of Arab leaders, their radio, and newspapers, and the remembered
threats of the Nazis: we had entered into a *Shoah* (holocaust) psychosis, all
around us enemies threatening us with extermination and having both the
means and the will to carry out their threat. As the ring closed in and help
seemed far, one noticed one's neighbors who had been in Auschwitz and
Bergen-Belsen going about white-faced. It was all too obvious what was the
source of their dread. The years in between had momentarily fallen away,
and they were back in that veritable nightmare world. The dark night of the
soul was upon us. *And it was the commandment which the Lord of history
had, so to speak, pronounced at Auschwitz which saved us.* I told my friend
that I could not entirely accept his explanation because I knew that a
majority of the soldiers had no personal or family recollections of the Euro-
pean holocaust: they had come from North Africa or Yemen, or even the
neighboring Arab countries where at that time such horrors were unknown.
How could they feel the force of the analogy as could the survivors of Buch-
enwald? He told me that the intervening twenty years had brought it about
that the holocaust had become a collective experience pressing consciously
and unconsciously on the minds of all, even the young, for whom Jewish
history in the Diaspora had come to an end with the beginnings of Israeli
independence [my italics].

5. *Judaism,* Summer 1967, pp. 272ff.
6. See note 4.
7. For a fuller discussion of many of the ideas merely hinted at in this brief essay,
   see my *Quest For Past and Future: Essays in Jewish Theology* (Bloomington;
   Indiana University Press, 1968), particularly the opening essay.

TRANSCENDENCE AND "COSMIC CONSCIOUSNESS"

HENRY NELSON WIEMAN

MANY INFLUENTIAL THINKERS today are engaged in reinterpreting religion. Two concepts involved in the discussion are "Transcendence" and "cosmic consciousness."

All religious commitment to creativity involves Transcendence. The question is, Transcendence in what sense? The present inquiry will show in what sense commitment to creativity involves Transcendence, and also those interpretations of Transcendence which are rejected by this commitment.

TRANSCENDENCE

It is not denied here that the creativity we have been describing *may* be the manifestation in human existence of transcendent being. But there are several objections to directing our ruling commitment to what transcends the creativity operating in human existence. Some of these are the following:

1. Our first responsibility is to make of human existence the best that is possible, and this we can do only by total commitment to what operates in human existence.

2. If this creativity is the manifestation in human existence of transcendent being, then our commitment to this creativity is also a commitment to this transcendent being and nothing more is required.

3. When we give priority to that which transcends this creativity, we divert our commitment from that alone which can save and carry human existence to its ultimate attainment.

4. What transcends the reach of human knowledge must either

153

be falsified by imposing on it the categories of the human mind, or given symbols that provide no descriptive knowledge of it. In neither case can it guide us in making major decisions.

5. More serious than any of the above is the last objection. When commitment is directed to what transcends the creativity which is open to scientific inquiry, religious inquiry cannot join with the sciences because transcendent being is beyond the reach of scientific research. Consequently other agencies, not concerned with the salvation and creative transformation of human existence, will take over this supreme instrument of power and shape human life to serve their ends. This will bring human life to an end after a period of fear, hate, torture, and tyranny.

This will be our fate because the power of science has become so great that if it is not used to serve the creativity that saves, it will obstruct this creativity so that it cannot save.

These are the objections to directing the ruling commitment of human existence to any being that transcends the creativity operating in human existence. We turn now to examining the kind of Transcendence involved in creativity itself.

This creativity operates by way of a creative interchange of symbolized meanings; and symbolized meanings subject to this creativity expand indefinitely the range of what men can know, control, and value. In this sense it is open toward infinity.

However, human existence is not able to carry this creativity to infinity, not because symbolized meanings are unfit to extend infinitely, but because the material and organic conditions of human existence prevent it from undergoing the continuous creativity beyond all limits and hence to infinity.[1]

When we recognize that human existence, despite its limitations, is the carrier of symbolized meanings capable of infinite expansion, we find that we have in our lives the potentiality for infinite value, knowledge, and power. We cannot in our own existence fully actualize this potential, but we are the carriers of a creativity that has this potential. Therefore, when we become fully aware of the significance of this creativity, we have the experience of what has been called the *mysterium tremendum*. We are unfit to be the carriers of this potential glory and power, unfit in the sense that we cannot carry it to the complete actualization of its potentiality. But we can live in it and for it and by means of it, to the degree to which we commit ourselves to it and repent of whatever we do in willful departure from its demands. It may generate in us fear, awe, and wonder; fear because of our inability to meet its demands fully; awe because of the grandeur of what might be if we could carry it to infinity; wonder because of the glimpses we see of what it might accomplish.

The human organism can carry this creativity to a certain point. To carry it farther would require a restructuring of the organism that biological existence does not permit. Awareness of this unattainable reach of creativity is experience of the holy.

It is obvious that this experience can very readily be misinterpreted as the manifestation in human life of a transcendent being in whom all the potentialities of this creativity are fully actualized. But when we make such a claim we go beyond the evidence. All we can say with assurance is that symbolized meanings have this potentiality when continuously and fully subjected to creative interchange. It is the zest and glory of life to be the carrier of this creativity: it is the humility of life to recognize that we cannot carry it to that infinity toward which it is open; it is the shame of our lives to recognize that so much of our time and energy are willfully given to goals that obstruct and defeat the working of this creativity; it is the wisdom of our lives to recognize that, to the degree to which we refuse to live for this creativity, we are moving toward our own self-destruction. The tragedy of our lives is that what might have been is so far from what actually is; much of the misery and suffering in our lives is involved in this departure from what we ought to be.

This is the kind of Transcendence involved in religious commitment to the creativity operating in human existence. It is in contrast to the kind of Transcendence attributed to a perfect being in whom all the potentialities of this creativity are eternally and completely actualized. Even if there is such a being, we fail to find the best that human existence can attain if we do not commit ourselves to the creativity operating in our lives.

Since religion throughout the Western world, and also in many other parts of the world, has been understood to be commitment to God, who is variously interpreted, issues will be clarified if we note the characteristics creativity has in common with "God" and the characteristics in which it differs.

Following are nine characteristics which creativity has in common with what is commonly given the name of "God."

1. Creativity produces the humanity of the individual when "humanity" means a valuing consciousness capable of indefinite expansion.

2. Creativity produces our humanity throughout the course of history.

3. Creativity saves our humanity from its destructive and degenerative propensities when the required conditions are met, doing this for the individual in his own life, and for the human race throughout the course of history.

4. Creativity produces a community of mutual support and mutual understanding between the widest ranges of diversity.

5. Creativity produces the freedom of the individual to develop his own unique individuality, when the required conditions are present.

6. Creativity creates the universe as known to the human mind.

7. Creativity presents human history, so far as history carries the potentialities of increasing value.

8. Creativity transforms human existence toward the greatest content of value that human existence can embody, when the required conditions are met.

9. Creativity should be served above all else by all men throughout human history, to the end of their salvation and creative transformation.

Following are nine characteristics attributed to "God" which do not apply to the creativity operating in human existence.

1. A supernatural person or a person of any kind.

2. Creator of the universe prior to, and independent of, the human mind.

3. Operates beyond the kinds of existence which live by symbolized meaning capable of indefinite expansion.

4. A cosmic mind.

5. The pantheistic totality of all existence.

6. Eternal and infinite being transcending all forms of existence.

7. The mystery of being beyond the reach of human knowledge.

8. Ideals most inclusive of all values. (Some identify God with this.)

9. Human striving after highest ideals. (Dewey identifies God with this.)

After distinguishing the kind of transcendence involved in commitment to creativity from other kinds, we turn now to examine the interpretation of the religious commitment set forth by the followers of Alfred North Whitehead. This is required to clarify the interpretation defended here. However, it is necessary for another reason. I spent several years studying Whitehead's intricate and complicated system with the hope of learning from this great thinker the best available interpretation of religious commitment. But after years of study and critical thinking I reached the conclusion that Whitehead's is not the kind of commitment fitted to save man from his self-defeating propensities and to transform him toward the best that human life can attain. I have, therefore, rejected the Whiteheadian answer to the basic religious question, although I have learned much from this great man. This indebtedness to Whitehead might lead to confusion if distinctions are not clearly drawn between the teaching of those who follow Whitehead and the commitment to creativity as interpreted here.

"COSMIC CONSCIOUSNESS"

The idea of God set forth in the philosophy of Whitehead has been modified by a number of philosophers and theologians to bring it into more accord with traditional Christianity. Among these are Charles Hartshorne, Schubert Ogden, John Cobb, and Paul Weiss. We shall take the thought of Charles Hartshorne as representative of this group. Although they do not all agree in every respect, they are sufficiently alike to take one as representative of the others.

According to Hartshorne, the cosmos is God's body and this body has a "cosmic consciousness" that is the mind of God. With various modifications, this view is in general accepted by the followers of

Whitehead. Since all the galactic systems, with their exploding stars and vast lifeless spaces in between, give no evidence of being organized like a biological organism fit to embody a conscious mind, this view is not accepted here. The writer finds it indefensible. However, in the following criticism we will pass over this lack of evidence for belief in a "cosmic consciousness" and will examine the fitness of such a being (supposing that it actually exists) for commanding the religious commitment of our lives.

We put quotation marks about "cosmic consciousness" to indicate that, in our opinion, no such being actually exists, that it is an idea examined for its religious significance.

Defenders of the belief in "cosmic consciousness" claim that it exercises supreme control over the total cosmos; but that it is not omnipotent in the sense of depriving innovating events of all power and initiative of their own. Consequently there can be much evil in existence, when evil means processes and forms of existence that are opposed to the values of this "cosmic consciousness." This point does not contravene the religious idea of God. We mention it only to pass on to other characteristics of this "cosmic consciousness."

Our criticism will show that all the highest values of human existence, by which and for which we live, are evil from the standpoint of the "cosmic consciousness" because they run counter to the values such a being must have. This is contrary to the claim of the writers we are criticizing and it is the central point of dispute between us.

This opposition between the good of "cosmic consciousness" and human good becomes apparent when we analyze the nature of what the good of "cosmic consciousness" must be when it has the cosmos as its body. This opposition between human good and the good of "cosmic consciousness" demonstrates that the latter cannot be God in the religious meaning of this word because "God" is defined as one who sustains the highest values of human life.

Our argument might be stated thus: There is no cosmic consciousness, but if there were one, it must necessarily be of such a nature that it cannot command the religious commitment of our lives, and therefore has not the value attributed to it by giving it the name of "God."

Our argument is not that the material universe is opposed to human values; it is merely indifferent to them. The material universe is serving as material to be organized into a system sustaining our values, or left out of such a system, as the case may be. But when the cosmos is said to have a conscious purpose of its own, this indifference becomes opposition. For example, if I fall from a height and am killed, I cannot say that gravitation is opposed to me, since it has no conscious purpose.

Another possible misunderstanding should be removed. This opposition between the values of human life and the values of the "cosmic mind" should not be confused with the teaching of the Hebrew and Christian prophets who have often declared that what men seek as good is evil in the sight of God. The prophets were condemning those strivings in human life which are opposed to love and justice. It is precisely the values of love and justice that run counter to the values of the "cosmic consciousness." The latter recognizes no values other than satisfactions experienced in its own body, because nothing exists outside of its own body. Love and justice are not values experienced in one's own body, like the taste of food and drink and other sensuous pleasures. Love and justice are experienced in the relations between persons. Since the "cosmic consciousness" has no interest in anything outside its own body, it can have no experience of love and justice.

To show the extent of the error involved in giving the name of "God" to a "cosmic consciousness," analysis of the idea as presented by its advocates must be carried further.

This "cosmic consciousness" has allegedly been in supreme control of the cosmos throughout time. Yet nowhere throughout the vast expanses of the cosmos has this supreme control allowed evolution to produce individuals who seek values outside their own bodies, except on rare planets that are infinitesimal specks compared to the total cosmos. Scientists speculate that other planets like ours may sustain a human kind of existence, although we have no knowledge of them. Probably there are such planets; but even if there are millions of them, their number, compared to all of the great star galaxies and the spaces between the galaxies, is infinitesimal. Even on this planet human life has appeared only very recently and is a very small part of the myriad forms of other life such as plants, insects, microbes, and so forth. These have no sense of love and justice, history and society, science, philosophy, and religion. Human life, in contrast to all other forms of life, has these values; but only since civilization began has human life begun to dominate the earth. Even so, human life is minute in quantity and brief in time compared to atoms and molecules and other lower forms of life. Furthermore, all life on this planet is doomed to extinction after existing a lifetime that is scarcely an instant when compared to endless time.

All this shows that the "cosmic mind" does not permit evolution issuing in human values to arise except in spots of time and space so limited as to seem, from the standpoint of this "cosmic consciousness," like aberrations and evils. This is further reason for saying that it is unfit to be revered as God.

According to those who identify God with "cosmic consciousness," even the smallest unit of existence has a subjective aim which it seeks to attain. In this sense it has values even though it may not be conscious. Let us call these smallest units "atomic events." Each atomic event absorbs (prehends) influences from other atomic events which it appropriates in seeking to fulfill its own subjective aim, analogous to the biological organism appropriating food and air to keep itself alive. But each atom makes this contribution to other atoms only after it perishes. During its own existence each atomic event seeks only the satisfaction of its own subjective aim without contributing anything to other atomic events until after it ceases to exist. Thus each atomic event seeks only the satisfaction of its own body and is not concerned with any other kind of value. In this it is like the total "cosmic consciousness," seeking no values other than values experienced in its own body.

The contribution which every atomic event makes to the subjective aim of other atomic events after its own death is due to the way the cosmos is ordered by the "cosmic being." Therefore it is perpetrated by the "cosmic mind" to satisfy the needs of its own body; there is no concern for anything outside its own body because there is nothing outside its own body.

This demonstrates that the "cosmic mind," together with everything under its control (except a few rare aberrations such as human existence), is concerned with no values outside the satisfactions of the body, called here the "subjective aim." Only in human life do we find a turning outward for values beyond the self, in the lives of others in society and in history. Some of the higher animals may show the faint beginning of seeking values outside the body of the individual, but it is difficult to know how much of this is instinct and conditioning, therefore, demands of the body rather than a recognition of objective values. In any case, no form of life except the human has the kind of language fit to carry symbolized meanings creatively toward infinity.

Even in human life values are experienced as bodily feelings, but these feelings represent objects of value outside the body, such as persons loved; the developments of history before and after the life of the individual; the hopes and fears, joys and sorrows of other people beyond the self; the expanding scope of knowledge; scenes of beauty and works of art. In short, the values sustaining human existence are the values of a culture carried through history by symbolized meanings representing a world of values extending far beyond the body of the individual, consciously shared by him with society and successive generations. Values of this kind require language (symbolized meanings) possessed by no other form of life of which we have knowledge. Atoms and molecules pervading the total cosmos and constituting almost the whole of its content have no such values. Even human beings struggle at times against the driving force pervading the rest of organic life, trying to ignore the complex demands of society and history.

In comparison with the values which sustain human existence, the "cosmic consciousness" is so extreme a sensualist that it could not be tolerated in human society; it does not respond to any person, cause, or object outside its own body. Neither does this "cosmic consciousness," throughout the vast reaches of time and space under its control, support the form of evolution producing the values of human existence, except at points so rare in space and time as to seem like innovations contrary to the ruling purpose of this "cosmic mind." This impression is further supported when we note that human existence is fated to become extinct after a relatively brief period of existence. According to the teaching of modern science, eventually the sun will explode and destroy all life in the solar system.

We conclude that "cosmic consciousness" cannot be worshiped as

God because it can be neither the lure of our aspirations, the guide and support of human striving, nor our savior from the ways of evil. Our ruling commitment must be given to what creates and sustains love and justice, beauty and truth, courage and human power or control. It must not be given to a "cosmic consciousness" which obstructs the evolution of these values by keeping the giant stars so hot that no such evolution is possible on them or near them, or in the vast spaces between the stars, or on the planets of which we have knowledge. On our planet the evolution leading to human values has been only a single branch of evolution, precariously maintained amidst other forms of life and material conditions; and only since the beginning of agriculture has human life begun to dominate the planet. Even now atoms and molecules, with their "subjective aims," comprise almost the entire content of the earth; and with their nuclear energy they threaten the continued existence of the symbolized meanings which carry all the distinctively human values.

We further conclude that whether or not we give the name of "God" to what commands the ruling commitment of our lives, we must not commit ourselves to a "consciousness" that has the cosmos for its body. Instead we must commit ourselves to what expands indefinitely the range of values we can share in community with others by transforming subhuman processes into a system support- ing the values by which and for which we live. The "cosmic con- sciousness," supposing that it exists, is opposed to all this by reason of the nature attributed to it, and should therefore be excluded from religious concern.

REFERENCES

1. We can of course at any time mathematically symbolize an infinity of infinities; but what is meant here is an unlimited expansion in the range of what men might know, value, and control. Symbolized meanings are of such a nature that this unlimited expansion could occur if human existence were able to carry these meanings beyond every limit in structuring the infinite fullness of being. Structuring means specific values, true statements, and activities of control so ordered and multiplied as to expand a single valuing consciousness to infinity. The fiction of a divine consciousness has been represented in this way. This

fiction has haunted the minds of men because human beings are the carriers of symbolized meanings that could structure infinite being in this way if human existence were able to undergo the required transformation. The creativity operating in human existence can expand the valuing consciousness indefinitely, but not to infinity.

DIVINE ABSOLUTENESS AND DIVINE RELATIVITY

CHARLES HARTSHORNE

FROM THE WORSHIPFULNESS belonging by definition to God it has been customary to deduce his "unlimitedness" or absolute infinity—and indeed the whole of the negative theology. But this deduction, as I and others have argued, is fallacious. What really follows is the unsurpassability of God, not his sheer infinity or absoluteness. Anselm almost discovered this when he defined God as such that a greater or better cannot be conceived. He "almost" discovered it, for there is an ambiguity in his definition, and he implicitly resolved the ambiguity in what I take to be the wrong way—that is, so as to make unsurpassability coincide with infinity, or the notion of a *ne plus ultra,* and thus to entail the negative theology.

This theology I regard as a religious heresy largely attributable to the presitge of Greek thought. The ambiguity can, however, be resolved so as to permit a clear distinction between worshipfulness and infinity, or between God and "the absolute." To be worthy of worship a being must not be (conceivably) surpassed *by another,* but he need not, in all respects, be unsurpassable absolutely, for it may, indeed it must, in some respects be *self*-surpassable. Is there any logical rule by which one may deduce the possibility of being surpassed by others from that of self-surpassing? True, for some modes of self-surpassing the inference would hold; for instance, if a weak being becomes strong or an evil being good. These modes of self-surpassing are therefore implicitly denied in denying the possibility of being surpassed by another.

But, as I am almost weary of pointing out to my fellow philosophers, there are other modes of self-surpassing. A being may in certain respects be finite or capable of increase, and yet it may be incon-

ceivable that another should surpass the being. Suppose the finitude is the finitude of actuality as a whole, and that this relation is a
necessary one, i.e., that the very individual identity of the being
involves its being all-inclusive. Ordinary beings are individuated by
their particular fragmentary roles in existence, by the way in which
each one is an included rather than an all-inclusive reality. The worshipful being, on the contrary, is individuated by its unique all-
inclusiveness. This is the attribute of "ubiquity" or "immensity,"
long ago recognized but not perhaps properly construed. If this is
conceivable, God cannot be less than all-inclusive, and hence it is a
contradiction to think of him as surpassed by another, no matter
how he may surpass himself, for the other could not be more than
one of his own fragments. Not finitude but fragmentariness is the
mark of the nondivine. Hundreds of thousands of scholars have
managed to miss this distinction.

It is manifest that this scheme will work only if the whole of
things is thought of as capable of increase, and for this reason a
theist should reject the modern Parmenideanism which takes reality to be a timeless totality of which temporal events are parts. Also,
"divine" must no longer be taken to entail "immutable." The
Greek exaltation of eternity and disparagement of time is one
thing, worship is another.

Can a being which is necessarily all-inclusive be personal? I have
not seen a valid argument to the contrary. Granted a person must
relate himself to another, does it follow that the other must be "outside" his own reality? Trinitarians by implication rejected this
dogma, and Fechner long ago argued explicitly and with care
against it. The "other" must be nonidentical with the all-
surpassing, all-including reality, but "X includes Y" not only does
not entail that X and Y are identical, it rather entails their non-
identity. Genuine or "proper" relations—and inclusion can be genuine—are between nonidentical terms. "X includes X" is a
"degenerate case." Fechner (following and clarifying Lotze and
Schelling) also argued carefully for the view that inclusion in the
divine life does not conflict with creaturely freedom.

I hold that he was right. God includes us by knowing us, and it
inheres in the very meaning of knowledge that it does not deter-

mine but accepts its objects. What the knower determines is his response to objects, which must be already determinate or there is nothing to know. Not that we could be what we are without God, but that the power of God over us consists in his being the supreme object of our awareness (largely unconscious, not knowledge in the fullest sense). God influences us by letting us be aware of him rather than simply by his awareness of us.

True, the importance of God for us as our supreme object arises from his uniquely adequate awareness of us (we love him because he first loved us); but God as influencing me *now* is God as knowing me as I have been, not as I am now. God as knowing me as I am now will not influence *that* state of me. The model of influence is the dialogue. I speak, you listen; then you speak and I listen. Buber was right: there is nothing higher than the I-thou relation. But in this relation there is always a time difference between stimulus and response; indeed responses are the only stimuli. And knowledge is simply the adequate response.

Clearly "power" conceived on this model is in principle relative, not absolute. "Absolute power" is meaningless or contradictory. It would amount to this: God "makes" our decisions in their full detail and concreteness. But then the only genuine decisions are God's. This is not even tyranny; it is nonsense. And the classical problem of evil is the exploitation of this nonsense. Evils are not and could not be what God inflicts upon us; they are what creatures inflict upon each other and also upon God, who has to accept them as objects of his knowledge. In this sense God is "the fellow sufferer who understands" (Whitehead). This I take to be the meaning of the cross, a meaning which even Christians have scarcely accepted. God's power is not absolute, but it is unsurpassable. No conceivable being could have more power. But any power must stop short of fully determining the others. Phrases like *creatio ex nihilo* do not abolish this other's necessity.

A source of confusion is the following reasoning: God is not free to choose between deciding rightly and deciding wrongly, yet surely God is free if anyone is. So why should God not make us free, yet incapable of evil? Here are several confusions. I agree with the main tradition that God can only decide rightly. But to suppose it follows that God's actions are necessitated, that he is a spiritual automaton, is remarkably arbitrary. Ethical principles are "not the sort of things" from which particular actions follow. In Kant for instance the only perfectly definite duties are negative, telling us what is not to be done, while the positive duties are broad abstractions, such as: promote the welfare of others, or cultivate your own talents.

Being necessitated to these modes of action would still leave one with innumerable free decisions to make. God would be more, not less free, since his range of creative capacities is unsurpassable, whereas ours is surpassable. An unimaginative person sees fewer optional alternatives under the imperative, "promote the happiness of others," than an imaginative or creative one. Virtue is only a formal framework of action, not its concrete specificity.

But still, if virtue can be necessitated, why did God not create us, like himself, free but necessarily virtuous beings? First of all, because it is not merely for the sake of ethical freedom that creatures are free. The basic significance of freedom is aesthetic (our metaphysics has been too obsessed with moral questions to see this) and the need for freedom is universal to life or sentience. Indeed, for a psychicalist like the present writer (or various scientists and philosophers) it is meaningless to speak of invididuals, even atomic or subatomic, whose concrete actions are necessitated, or specified in advance by antecedent conditions. Only the abstract can be so specified, and virtue can in God be necessary only because of its abstract character.

The concrete values are aesthetic, not ethical, as Kant clearly saw and we all should never forget. The particular actual beauty of the cosmos for God is contingent, and in continual process of accretion, and hence the value of his actual experience is likewise endlessly enriched. (This does not make God surpassable in any sense that is incompatible with worship; for no being could be other than contingent and capable of increase in the concrete value of its experiences.)

In the second place, the possibility of necessary virtue in God does not refute the explanation of evil—both natural and, as we shall see presently, moral—through the freedom of the creatures. This is so for two reasons. Natural evil is explained not solely by moral freedom but by the aesthetic freedom inherent in all experience as such, whether on the rational or ethical plane or not. Whitehead is one of the few philosophers who have seen this. It is the point of his "category of the ultimate," creativity. The risk of evil is inherent in multiple individuality since this means multiple freedom or self-determination (the "self-created creature," an idea not invented by Whitehead, or Sartre either). The risk is worthwhile, since multiple freedom is the condition of any opportunity for good. This solution of the problem of evil has been repeatedly stated, though mostly quite recently, but it is missed "as if by magic" by most writers. Nor does it make God surpassable by another; for no being could have content for its experience in mere solitude, nor could it escape solitude by completely controlling its "others," for a completely controlled individual is no individual.

In the third place, as to moral evil, God "failed" to make us, like himself, free unsurpassably, only as between good and good, simply because such necessary virtue is the unsurpassable form of freedom and, like the other aspects of unsurpassability, necessarily unique to God himself.

Concerning the frequently alleged need of the worshiper to believe in "omnipotence" in order to feel wholly safe in the hands of God, I can only submit that the longing for security is one thing, worship another. Worship is well defined as "loving God with all one's being." This does not entail, though it is plausible to think it entails, the idea that no harm can befall the one who does this. Absolute security against suffering, for instance, cannot (if some of us see aright) be attributed even to the worshipful being itself, let alone to its worshipers. (I say "its" not to avoid the personal but to avoid the sexual—ordinary language being genuinely deficient at this point.)

The all-knowing knows suffering too, and this is logically impossible without in some sense suffering oneself. To love is to see one's own good in the other's, to love with all one's being (i.e., worship) is to see all one's good in the good of the Other. And only the One who appreciates all creaturely values—as no creature can do—can achieve a good inclusive of everyone's good. For this reason the creatures can properly locate all their good in, i.e., can worship, the divine good.

The worshipful must be supposed omnipotent in whatever sense all-powerfulness is a conceivable property which would render its possessor superior to a nonomnipotent being, but in no other sense. The antinomies into which customary interpretations of the term lead us constitute warnings against accepting these constructions as derived from worshipfulness. For the latter only requires that another more powerful being must not be conceivable. Moreover, if it is nonsense, as I hold it is, that one being should literally make the concrete decisions of another—for they would then be the decisions of the first being only, not of the second—the unsurpassable form of conceivable power cannot be a sheer monopoly of power, rendering others powerless to make any decisions of their own.

The higher forms of power are not those which inhibit the freedom of others, but rather those which inspire appropriate degrees and kinds of freedom in them, the power of artists, prophets, men of genius, and true statesmen. God is the unsurpassable inspiring genius of all freedom, not the all-determining coercive tyrant, or (if possible) even worse, the irresistible hypnotist who dictates specific actions while hiding his operations from the hypnotized. The worship of power in any such sense is idolatry in a rather brutal form. The admirable rulers are not those who try to make all decisions themselves, but those who put others in a position to make fruitful decisions of their own. As Berdyaev says, the divine imperative to us is not mechanical obedience to ready-made or eternal divine decisions, but creative response to the divine creativity: be creative and foster creativity in others.

The view that God is not the wholly unsurpassable absolute, but rather the inclusive reality surpassable only by itself in later phases, has many advantages besides that of making room for freedom and eliminating the "problem of evil."

1. It enables us to take seriously the idea that we should love God with *all* our being, and yet also love our neighbor as truly as we love ourselves. For suppose God is wholly absolute: it follows that he is totally independent of what happens to us and our neighbor, from which it follows that the divine actuality does not include us. (For no whole can be entirely independent of its constituents. If there is such a thing as relativity, a whole or inclusive reality is relative to its included constituents.) It follows further that that aspect of our

being which loves one's neighbor (or oneself) is directed not to God but to something external to Him. We are loving God and, as an additional love, our neighbor. But then our *whole* being is not constituted by love of God. Only if the neighbor, and everything in which we take even the faintest interest, is included in God can our love for God be the whole of our being. I infer, as I take Paul Tillich to have inferred, that we must be included within the reality of God. But it also follows that God is not entirely independent of us, since a constituent must make some difference to the whole which includes it.

2. If God were simply immutable, our interest in the future and in possibilities for creating new values would be a religious impertinence. The will to create values makes religious sense only if God himself can be enriched by such creation.

3. Although God as inclusive must be relative to the included creatures, our doctrine allows us nevertheless to employ the term "absolute" as a divine attribute. Absolute means nonrelative, independent of others; it also implies immutability. As including his creatures God is relative and mutable, for each new creature gives him new qualifications. (And the creatures, using their freedom, limited though it is, decide something about what God is to be.) Yet this does not, by any rule of logic, prevent God from having aspects which are independent of and unchangeable by the creatures. Indeed, if God is unsurpassable by another, this property itself must be viewed as independent and immutable. For, were it to change, he could be surpassed by another; hence such change is contradictory. So we can say, with so many of our ancestors, "God is absolute"; we need only add, "but not in all respects." God has aspects of immutability or strict independence; he has also aspects of changeability or relativity. I call this the "principle of dual transcendence." For no individual who is not God is in any aspect independent of all others, so that God's independence transcends ordinary independence; but equally, no individual other than God is in any aspect inclusive of, and so relative to, *all* others. The divine independence and divine dependence are thus equally distinctive. In a similar way, not to be explained here, God can be said to be both finite and infinite.

4. Holding this view, we can take seriously the idea that God is the eminently loving Being. To love another is not simply to do good to the other; it is to care agout his weal and woe, to share in his joys and sorrows. The sun does good but loves not. Is this the right model for theology? To love another is to allow his fortunes to make a difference to us, and this is relativity, if words continue to have meaning. So a merely absolute God cannot love. Many thinkers have pointed this out. But a merely relative God cannot love eminently. For the eminence itself must be an absolute property. Always, necessarily, and immutably divine love is unsurpassable—yes, even by God himself, simply *qua* love. God does not grow more loving; He is already the ideal of love. But His satisfaction in the creation grows, for He has additional creatures to love. I believe the possibility of this distinction is implicit in the meaning of love in any form. We contribute, not to the divine character, his perfect love or righteousness, but to the divine satisfaction—if you will, his happiness. And to make this contribution as best we may is our end and aim, if we understand ourselves.

Instead of allowing a foolish overestimation of independence or immutability to limit the possibility that God is love, we can say that God is absolute and immutable in just those respects that love permits and requires, and he is relative and mutable in just those other respects that love also permits and requires. Then we can be intellectually honest without repudiating the highest intuitions of our religious heritage.

There is a conviction which I have long had: for every trap into which an anti-theist falls there is a respected theist (or a hundred) who has led him into that trap. Or, to put it otherwise, God's professed friends, like professed friends generally, may sometimes be more dangerous to his cause than professed enemies. It is easy to say, Lord, Lord, but not so easy to serve the Lord wisely and well. God's view of the opponents of theism is not likely to resemble very closely that of the conventionally pious defenders of this doctrine.

NOTES ON CONTRIBUTORS

Robert N. Bellah is Ford Professor of Sociology and Comparative Studies at the University of California. He is the author of *Tokugawa Religion* and, more recently, *Beyond Belief: Essays on Religion in a Post-Traditional World.*

Harvey Cox has written *The Secular City, On Not Leaving It to the Snake,* and *A Feast of Fools,* and is professor of church and society at the Harvard Divinity School.

Donald Cutler has edited *The Religious Situation: 1968, The Religious Situation: 1969,* and *Updating Life and Death: Essays in Ethics and Medicine.* He is presently editor of religious books at Harper and Row.

Emil L. Fackenheim is the author of *Quest for Past and Future: Essays in Jewish Theology* and *The Religious Dimension in Hegel's Thought,* among other books. He is professor of philosophy at the University of Toronto and a contributing editor of the journal *Judaism.*

Charles Hartshorne is professor of philosophy at the University of Toronto. He has written *Beyond Humanism: Essays in the Philosophy of Nature, Divine Relativity,* and other books.

Gordon D. Kaufman is professor of theology at the Harvard Divinity School. Among his books are *Relativism, Knowledge and Faith,* and *Systematic Theology: A Historicist Perspective.*

Sam Keen is at present professor of philosophy of the person at Prescott College and a consulting editor at *Psychology Today.* He is the author of *Gabriel Marcel, Apology for Wonder,* and *To a Dancing God.*

Michael Murphy is president of the Esalen Institute at Big Sur and San Francisco.

Herbert Richardson is an associate professor of theology at St. Michael's College of the University of Toronto, and is the author of *Toward an American Theology* and *Nun . . . Witch . . . Playmate: the Americanization of Sex.*

Donald Schon is the president of the Organization for Social and Technical Innovation, Inc., in Cambridge, Massachusetts.

Huston Smith, professor of humanities at the Massachusetts Institute of Technology, is the author of *Religions of Man*, among other works.

Henry Nelson Wieman, who lives in Grinnell, Iowa, is the dean of American liberal theologians. Among his books are *Man's Ultimate Commitment*, *Source of Human Good*, and *Religious Inquiry*.

INDEX

Abbott, Edwin: 13
Altizer, Thomas: 32, 35, 45, 46
American Labor Movement: 71, 72, 80
Apollo: 31–52 *passim*
Ardrey, Robert: 43
Aristotle: 58
Auschwitz: 147–151
Avicenna: 10
Axis mundi: 103, 104

Barth, Karl: 34, 98
Beckett, Samuel: 114
Bellah, Robert N.: 4, 13, 19
Benét, Stephen Vincent: 8
Benz, Ernst: 55
Berdyaev, Nikolai A.: 7, 169
Bergson, Henri: 2, 128
Bernanos, Georges: 7
Betrayal of the Body, The (Lowen): 27
Bloch, Ernst: 1, 7
Bohm, David: 10
Boisen, Anton: 21
Borton, Terry: 29
Brain, human: 15
Brown, Dr. George: 29
Brown, Norman O.: 32, 38, 40, 41, 45, 47–48
Bruner, Jerome S.: 105
Brunner, Emil: 35, 98
Buber, Martin: 114, 144, 146
Buddha: 4
Buddhism: 1–2
Bultmann: 115
Burke, Kenneth: 92

Castro, Fidel: 74
"Character armor": 27
Chu Hsi: 95
Cobb, John: 157
Cohen, Sidney: 16
Coleman, James: 12

Creativity: 153–157

Dabrowski, Dr. Kazinierz: 21
"Dead Sea scrolls": 56
Death: 14
"Deficiency needs" (Maslow): 87
Deism: 52
Demiurge: 33
Devil and Daniel Webster, The (Benét): 8
Dewey, John: 144
Diary of a Country Priest (Bernanos): 7
Dionysius: 31–52 *passim*
Dionysius the Areopagite: 10
Dualism, metaphysical-cosmological: 115, 130
Durkheim, Émile: 90

Eckhart, Meister: 4
Edwards, Jonathan: 88, 100–101
Ego: 31–32, 33, 36, 37, 41, 52
Eliot, T. S.: 102
Encounter groups: 18, 25
Erikson, Erik: 67
Esalen Institute (Big Sur, Cal.): 19, 25, 28, 29
Essene community: 56
Exploration into God (Robinson): 19
Exploration of the Inner World, The (Boisen): 21

Fackenheim, Emil: 74, 81
Fanon, Frantz: 74
Fechner, Gustav T.: 165
Feeling: anatomy of, 98–101
Ferré: 112
Flatland (Abbott): 13
Ford Foundation: 29
Freud, Sigmund: 86, 90; mythology, 36

INDEX

Genesis myth: 36
Gestalt therapy: 18, 26
God: Aristotelian concept of, 43
"God-language": 117–120, 133–135
Gomulka: 148
Goodman, Paul: 76, 82
Graham, Billy: 35
Growing Up Absurd (Goodman): 76, 82
Guatama: 3
Guevara, Ché: 74

Haldane, J. B. S.: 10
Hamlet: 81
Harrington, Michael: 53, 54
Hartshorne, Charles: 44, 157
Hegel, G. W. F.: 39, 145
Heidegger, Martin: 33, 38, 118, 146
Heim, Karl: 13
Heraclitus: 39
Heresy: 57
Hirai, Dr.: 23
Hitler, Adolf: 148, 150
Hoffer, Eric: 75
Homer: 111
Homo viator: 49
Hoyle, Fred: 13
Hubris: 36
Hume, David: 67
Huxley, Aldous: 19

Iconoclasm: 39
Id: 32, 36, 52
Image of the Future, The (Polak): 53
Images: 101–105
Immanence: 4–6
Island (Huxley): 19

James, William: 10, 17
Japan: and new religious development, 58
Jaspers, Karl: 39, 121
Jewish Values in the Post-Holocaust Future (symposium): 150

Kant, Immanuel: 144, 167
Katsamatsu, Dr.: 23
Kazantzakis, Nikos: 8, 32, 39
Kelly, Thomas: 99

Kierkegaard, Sören: 6, 7, 34
King, Martin Luther, Jr.: 148
Kubrick, Stanley: 111

Laing, Dr. R. D.: 19, 20, 69
Langley Porter Neuropsychiatric institute (San Francisco): 23
Language: 105; theological, 48, 121–123. See also "God-language"
Lankavatara Sutra: 5
Laski, Marghanita: 23
Lenski, Gerhard: 103
Limit, ultimate: 120–136
Litwak, Leo: 25–26
Lotze, Rudolf H.: 165
Lowen, Dr. Alexander: 26–28
"LSD and the Anguish of Dying" (Cohen): 16
Luther, Martin: 88

McLuhan, Marshall: 73, 77, 102
Maimonides: 10
Mania: 61
Marcel: 43, 48
Marcuse, Herbert: 32
Marx, Karl: 55, 144
Maslow, Abraham: 2, 19, 22, 87, 88
Mead, George Herbert: 78–79
Meditation: 18, 23
Mental hygiene: 60
Metz, Johannes: 59
Moltmann, Jurgen: 7
Morison, Elting: 66, 79
Morrison, Philip: 12
Munz, Peter: 4
Mysticism: 35, 38
Myth: 105
Myths: and signs, 104

Nagarjuna: 95
National Institute of Mental Health (Bethesda, Md.): 20
National Training Laboratories: 28
Nazi holocaust: 147–150
Net of Jewels: 19
Newberg, Norman: 29
New York Times Magazine: 25
Niebuhr, Reinhold: 35

INDEX

INDEX